# THE TOTALLY AMAZING
# FACT-PACKED, FOLD-OUT,
# ATLAS OF THE WORLD

**Picture Acknowledgements:**
The publishers would like to thank the following sources for their kind permission to reproduce the pictures in this book.

Key: t=Top, b=Bottom, c=Centre, l=Left and r=Right.
**6t** Thinkstock/Natalia Lukiyanova; **6bl** Getty Images/Digital Vision; **6br** Thinkstock/NAN104; **8tl** Alamy/© North Wind Picture Archives; **8bl** Corbis/©Paul A. Souders; **8r** Alamy/©Hemis; **9tl** Alamy/©canadabrian; **9tr** Shutterstock/Howard Sandler; **9b** Getty Images/Gordon Wiltsie; **10bl** Shutterstock/Songquan Deng; **10bc** Alamy/©Jonathan Larsen/Diadem Images; **10br** Getty Images/ Gustavo Caballero; **10t** Thinkstock/Stocktrek Images; **11t** Shutterstock/Chris Geszvain; **11b** Shutterstock/ karamysh; **14t** Shutterstock/Dr. Morley Read; **14bl** Shutterstock/Oleksiy Mark; **14br** Shutterstock/ Guido Amrein; **15l** Corbis/©Tom Bean; **15r** Shutterstock/Lee Prince; **16tl** Shutterstock/ChameleonsEye; **16tr** Shutterstock/meunierd; **16bl** Corbis/Nik Wheeler; **16br** Shutterstock/Brandon Bourdages; **17t** Shutterstock/Jo Ann Snover; **17b** Shutterstock/f9photos; **18** Shutterstock/Migel; **19l** Alamy/© Greg Balfour Evans; **19c** Corbis/Hemis/Christian Guy; **19r** Corbis/epa/Chico Sanchez; **20t** Shutterstock/ Sherjaca; **20c** Thinkstock/Renate Smitham; **20b** Shutterstock/easaab; **21t** The Bridgeman Art Library/ Private Collection; **21b** Shutterstock/NigelSpiers; **22l** Shutterstock; **22r** Alamy/© David Hodges; **23l** Shutterstock/Rusian Kerimov; **23c** Shutterstock/defpicture; **23r** Corbis/FLPA/Colin Marshall/Frank Lane Picture Library; **24t** Shutterstock/BartlomiejMagierowski; **24c** Shutterstock/SeanPavonePhoto; **24b** Shutterstock/Hung Chung Chih; **25t** Thinkstock/oksankash; **25c** Thinkstock/Ru Baile; **25b** iStockphoto/ EdStock; **26t** Thinkstock; **26r** Alamy/©ZUMA Press, Inc.; **26b** Thinkstock; **26l** Thinkstock/Anna Dudko; **27l** Thinkstock/©Sergey anatolievich Pristyazhnyuk; **27t** Thinkstock/David Cloud; **27r** Thinkstock/ Luciano Mortula; **28** Thinkstock/Fuse; **30l** Thinkstock/Zoonar; **30r** Thinkstock/Tersina Shieh; **31l** Getty Images/Richard I'Anson; **31t** Getty Images/Christopher Lee; **31b** Getty Images/Popperfoto; **32tl** Shutterstock/Zurijeta; **32tr** iStockphoto/EdStock; **32bl** Shutterstock/Waj; **32br** Shutterstock/ Protasov AN; **33l** Shutterstock/Patricia Hofmeester; **33r** Getty Images/Thomas J. Abercrombie; **34** Thinkstock/Anton Sokolov; **35l** Alamy/©ITAR-TASS Photo Agency; **35tr** Corbis/Xinhua Press/Ye Erjiang; **35br** Shutterstock/Serg Zastavkin; **36l** Shutterstock/Pichugin Dmitry; **36c** Shutterstock/LeonP; **36b** Shutterstock/Andrzej Kubik; **37l** Thinkstock/Photodynamic; **37r** Shutterstock/Elzbieta Sekowska; **38l** Shutterstock/sculpies; **38r** Thinkstock/Goodshoot; **39t** Shutterstock/Oleksandr Kalinichenko; **39l** Thinkstock/Trevor Kittelty; **39r** Getty Images/Robert Harding World Imagery/Godong; **39b** Shutterstock/ WitR; **40l** Getty Images/Eric Nathan; **40c** Shutterstock/Antonio Jorge Nunes; **40r** Alamy/©Images of Africa Photobank; **40t** Thinkstock/William Keith Wheatley; **41l** Alamy/© Allstar Picture Library; **41r** Shutterstock/capturefoto; **42tl** Shutterstock/Dan Breckwoldt; **42bl** Shutterstock/solarseven; **42br** Shutterstock/3renderings; **42tr** Science and Society Picture Library/National Railway Museum; **43l** Shutterstock/Burben; **43c** Thinkstock/Dieter Hawlan; **43r** Shutterstock/Slawomir Kruz; **46t** Shutterstock/ Vlada Z; **46c** Thinkstock/nevereverro; **46b** Thinkstock/mauribo; **47l** Shutterstock/Doin Oakenheim; **47r** Shutterstock/Vlada Z; **48t** Shutterstock/sippakorn; **48c** Shutterstock/javarman; **48b** Shutterstock/ Sergey Kelin; **49t** Shutterstock/Andrey Starostin; **49b** Shutterstock/Natursports; **50t** Corbis/San Francisco Chronicle/Brant Ward; **50c** Corbis/Demotix/Maciej Rozwadowski; **50b** Shutterstock/Nata Sdobnikova; **51t** Alamy/©epa european pressphoto agency b.v.; **51b** Shutterstock/littlewormy; **52t** Shutterstock/ Arto Hakola; **52bl** Corbis/Paul Souders; **52br** Shutterstock/Vlasimir Melnik; **53l** Corbis/Minden Pictures/ Tui de Roy; **53r** Shutterstock/BMJ; **54** Corbis/Ralph White; **55l** Getty Images/Science Photo Library/Jan Hinsch; **55r** Shutterstock/cdelacy.

Every effort has been made to acknowledge correctly and contact the source and/or copyright holder of each picture and Carlton Books Limited apologises for any unintentional errors or omissions, which will be, corrected in future editions of this book.

## THIS IS A CARLTON BOOK

Text, design and illustrations © Carlton Books Limited 2014, 2018

This edition published 2018 by Carlton Books Limited.
First published in 2014 by Carlton Books Limited,
an imprint of the Carlton Publishing Group
20 Mortimer Street, London W1T 3JW

A catalogue record for this book is available from the British Library.

ISBN: 978-1-78312-365-0

Printed and bound in Dubai

Executive editors: Selina Wood, Stephanie Stahl
Senior designer: Andrew Watson
Designers: Katie Baxendale, Amy McSimpson, Kate Wiliwinska
Map and editorial consultants: Craig Asquith, Marie Greenwood
Picture researcher: Emma Copestake
Publisher: Samantha Sweeney
Production: Ena Matagic, Emma Smart

# THE TOTALLY AMAZING
## FACT-PACKED, FOLD-OUT,
# ATLAS OF THE WORLD

Written by
**Jen Green**

Illustrated by
**Christiane Engel**

CARLTON KIDS

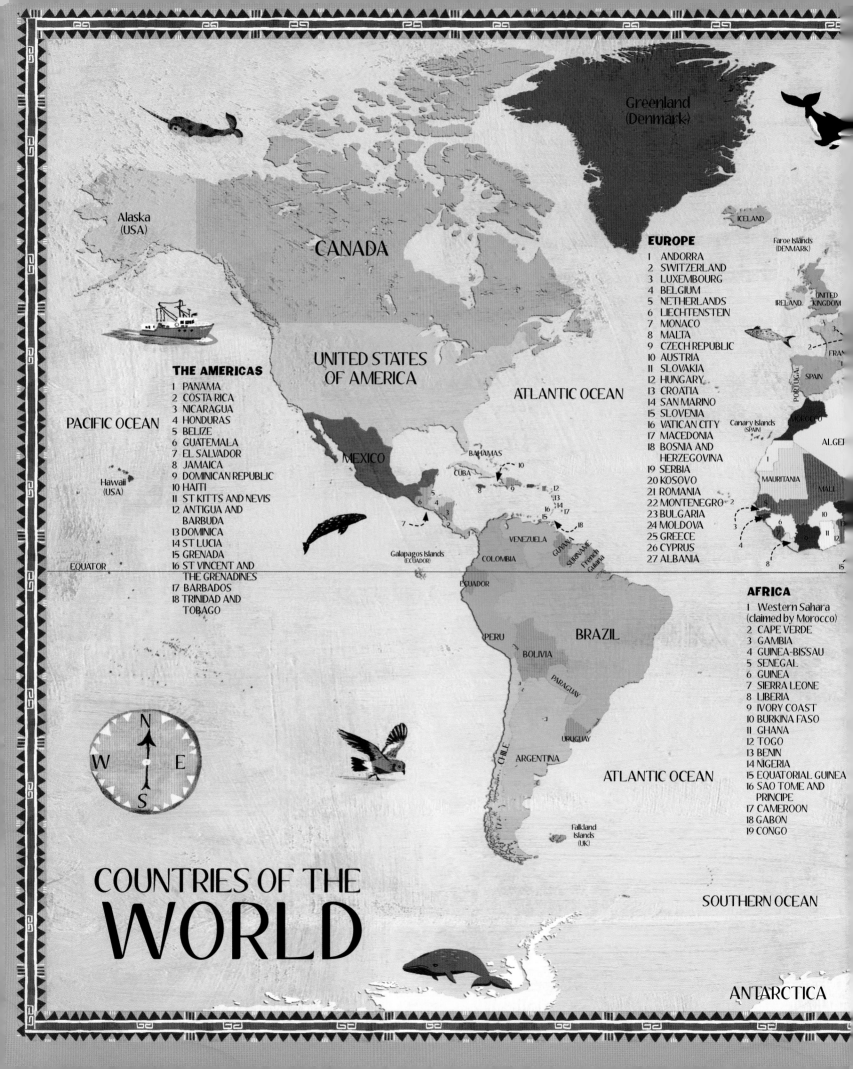

Greenland
(Denmark)

ICELAND

Alaska
(USA)

CANADA

Faroe Islands
(DENMARK)

**EUROPE**
1  ANDORRA
2  SWITZERLAND
3  LUXEMBOURG
4  BELGIUM
5  NETHERLANDS
6  LIECHTENSTEIN
7  MONACO
8  MALTA
9  CZECH REPUBLIC
10 AUSTRIA
11 SLOVAKIA
12 HUNGARY
13 CROATIA
14 SAN MARINO
15 SLOVENIA
16 VATICAN CITY
17 MACEDONIA
18 BOSNIA AND
   HERZEGOVINA
19 SERBIA
20 KOSOVO
21 ROMANIA
22 MONTENEGRO
23 BULGARIA
24 MOLDOVA
25 GREECE
26 CYPRUS
27 ALBANIA

IRELAND   UNITED
          KINGDOM

FRAN

PORTUGAL   SPAIN

Canary Islands
(SPAIN)

MOROCCO

ALGE

UNITED STATES
OF AMERICA

ATLANTIC OCEAN

**THE AMERICAS**
1  PANAMA
2  COSTA RICA
3  NICARAGUA
4  HONDURAS
5  BELIZE
6  GUATEMALA
7  EL SALVADOR
8  JAMAICA
9  DOMINICAN REPUBLIC
10 HAITI
11 ST KITTS AND NEVIS
12 ANTIGUA AND
   BARBUDA
13 DOMINICA
14 ST LUCIA
15 GRENADA
16 ST VINCENT AND
   THE GRENADINES
17 BARBADOS
18 TRINIDAD AND
   TOBAGO

PACIFIC OCEAN

Hawaii
(USA)

MEXICO

BAHAMAS

CUBA

1
MAURITANIA
MALI
2
5
3
4
6  9  10  11  13
8  12
15

Galapagos Islands
(ECUADOR)

VENEZUELA
COLOMBIA
GUYANA
SURINAME
French
Guiana

EQUATOR

ECUADOR

PERU

BOLIVIA

BRAZIL

PARAGUAY

**AFRICA**
1  Western Sahara
   (claimed by Morocco)
2  CAPE VERDE
3  GAMBIA
4  GUINEA-BISSAU
5  SENEGAL
6  GUINEA
7  SIERRA LEONE
8  LIBERIA
9  IVORY COAST
10 BURKINA FASO
11 GHANA
12 TOGO
13 BENIN
14 NIGERIA
15 EQUATORIAL GUINEA
16 SAO TOME AND
   PRINCIPE
17 CAMEROON
18 GABON
19 CONGO

URUGUAY

CHILE   ARGENTINA

ATLANTIC OCEAN

N
W   E
S

Falkland
Islands
(UK)

SOUTHERN OCEAN

# COUNTRIES OF THE
# WORLD

ANTARCTICA

ARCTIC OCEAN

RUSSIA

KAZAKHSTAN

MONGOLIA

UZBEKISTAN
KYRGYZSTAN
TURKMENISTAN
TAJIKISTAN

TURKEY

SYRIA
IRAQ
IRAN
AFGHANISTAN
PAKISTAN

NORTH
KOREA
SOUTH
KOREA
JAPAN

CHINA

EGYPT

SAUDI
ARABIA
OMAN
YEMEN

NEPAL
BHUTAN

BANGLADESH

INDIA

BURMA
(MYANMAR)
VIETNAM
LAOS

TAIWAN

PACIFIC OCEAN

SUDAN
ERITREA

SOUTH
SUDAN
ETHIOPIA
DJIBOUTI

SRI LANKA

THAILAND

CAMBODIA

PHILIPPINES

FEDERAL STATE
OF MICRONESIA

MARSHALL
ISLANDS

SOMALIA

INDIAN OCEAN

MALAYSIA

BRUNEI

PALAU

UGANDA
KENYA

MALDIVES

SINGAPORE

NAURU

KIRIBATI

BURUNDI

SEYCHELLES

INDONESIA

PAPUA NEW
GUINEA

TUVALU

TANZANIA

COMOROS

EAST
TIMOR

SOLOMON
ISLANDS

SAMOA

MALAWI

MADAGASCAR

MAURITIUS

VANUATU

FIJI

ZIMBABWE

MOZAMBIQUE

ASIA

1 GEORGIA
2 AZERBAIJAN
3 ARMENIA
4 LEBANON
5 ISRAEL
6 JORDAN
7 KUWAIT
8 BAHRAIN
9 QATAR
10 UNITED ARAB EMIRATES

TONGA

AUSTRALIA

SWAZILAND

LESOTHO

NEW ZEALAND

# CONTENTS

North America
(and Central
America) 8-17

Australia
(and New
Zealand) 20-21

Africa
36-41

Antarctica
And The Arctic
52-53

South America
13-14, 18-19

Asia
22-35

Europe
42-51

Oceans
(and Oceania)
54-55

# THE WORLD AT A GLANCE

Our Earth is one of eight planets circling our local star, the Sun. The Sun and all the planets, moons and rocks moving around it are called the Solar System. This is just one tiny part of an enormous star cluster called the Milky Way. Like the other planets close to the Sun, Earth is a rocky ball. It is mostly covered with ocean, which is why it looks blue from space. The dry land is shaped by waves and rivers, frost, ice and wind. Earth's continents and oceans are also shaped by tiny movements of sections of the Earth's outer crust which are called tectonic plates. Planet Earth supports the only life we know for certain exists in the Universe.

## INSIDE THE EARTH

Planet Earth formed as a ball of red-hot, molten rock some 4.6 billion years ago. Since then it has very slowly cooled, and the outer crust has hardened. But beneath the solid crust, the rock is still red-hot and semi-liquid. This molten rock bursts onto the surface when a volcano erupts. Earth's outer crust is made of giant plates that fit together like a globe-shaped jigsaw.

Red-hot inner core

Crust

A cross-section of the Earth.

Mantle (layer of hot rock).

## CLIMATE

Earth's climate varies from place to place. This is because different areas of the Earth get varying amounts of the Sun's heat, and also rainfall. The Sun's rays are strongest at the Equator (an imaginary line running around the middle of the Earth), and weakest at the Poles. Climate is also affected by height (mountains are cooler) and by the distance from the ocean. Areas far inland have a more extreme climate than places on the coast.

## LIVING PLANET

Life exists on Earth because of several crucial factors. Our planet is 150 million km away from the Sun – a distance that provides the perfect amount of heat and light for life to flourish. Earth's atmosphere contains oxygen, which animals need to breathe. As a ball of metal, Earth is magnetic. This magnetism helps to shield us from harmful space particles. The oceans provide water, which is also vital to life.

The Earth and neighbouring Moon.

Places near the Equator are hotter than elsewhere on Earth.

# CONTINENTS

Earth's dry land is divided into landmasses called continents. We say there are seven continents, although Asia and Europe are really one huge landmass. There are also thousands of islands, which are the tops of mountains and plateaus rising from the seabed.

North America

Europe    Asia

Africa

South America

Oceania

Antarctica

# CITIES

In 1900 only about 10 per cent of Earth's population lived in cities. Now over half of us live in urban areas. In many countries, city populations are growing fast, as people move from the countryside to find work.

# SEASONS

Earth tilts on its axis (an imaginary line between the North and South Pole) as it moves around the Sun. When the northern hemisphere leans towards the Sun it has summer. When it leans away it has winter. The opposite occurs in the southern hemisphere.

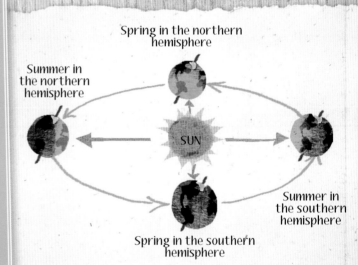

Spring in the northern hemisphere

Summer in the northern hemisphere

SUN

Summer in the southern hemisphere

Spring in the southern hemisphere

A chart showing the size of each continent, plus the percentage of the world's population living there.

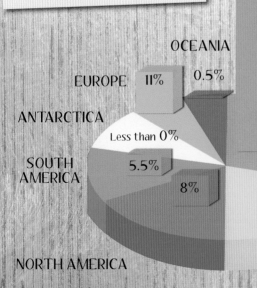

60%

ASIA

OCEANIA

EUROPE    11%    0.5%

ANTARCTICA

Less than 0%

SOUTH AMERICA    5.5%

8%    15%

NORTH AMERICA

AFRICA

# POPULATION

In 2012 Earth's population reached 7 billion – that is over four times the population in 1900. By 2040 there may be 9 billion people. Europe and parts of southern and eastern Asia are very densely populated. The polar regions and barren deserts have few or no people.

# NORTHERN NORTH AMERICA

The most northern region of North America is made up of Canada, Alaska and Greenland. Canada is a sweeping, rugged land and the world's second-largest country. The icy territory of Alaska is part of the USA (see p.10). Greenland, the world's largest island, belongs to Denmark (see p.42). The whole region has rich minerals, including coal, oil and natural gas. The far north is permanently snow-covered and few people live here. Most Canadians live in cities such as Toronto and Montreal, close to the border with the USA. In Alaska and Greenland, most people live near the coast.

(see p.10) ... (see p.42)

## EUROPEAN SETTLERS

Most Canadians are descendants of European settlers. From the 1600s, French and British merchants arrived in Canada to trade in the furs of animals such as the beaver. French and English are still the official languages of Canada. In the late 1800s, the discovery of gold in northwestern Canada brought many Europeans to the region.

## SPORTS

Ice hockey is one of the most popular sports in Canada. The sport is played at international level by both men and women. Skiing and skating are popular in winter, while summer sports include hiking, and sailing and canoeing in the country's lakes and rivers.

An ice hockey game in the Canadian province of Quebec.

Europeans traded with the existing native American inhabitants.

Forestry workers prepare to transport logs.

BEAUFORT SEA

Dog-pulled sledge

Timber

Alaska (USA)

Denali

CANADA

Mackenzie river

ROCKY MOUNTAINS

First Nation totem pole

Gas plant

PACIFIC OCEAN

Aleutian Islands

Canadian Pacific Railway

Vancouver

## FARMING

Wheat is grown on the prairies (large grassy plains) in southern Canada. Fruits such as apples and cherries ripen in orchards in sheltered valleys. Canada's evergreen forests yield timber for construction and woodpulp for paper. Maple trees produce sweet maple syrup. The maple leaf is a symbol of Canada and appears on the Canadian flag.

# USA

The United States of America (USA) is a large country made up of 50 states, 48 of which lie within one land mass between the Atlantic and the Pacific Oceans. The USA has varied landscapes, with snow-capped mountains in the west, plains in the centre, swamps in the southeast and deserts in the southwest. The remaining two states are Alaska and the Pacific islands of Hawaii. The USA has rich resources including forests, fertile farmlands and minerals such as iron ore, coal, oil and natural gas. It has very well-developed industries, and leads the world in manufacturing, electronics and computers. The USA is one of the world's richest countries, which gives it great power and influence. American trends in film and music also influence societies worldwide.

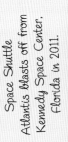

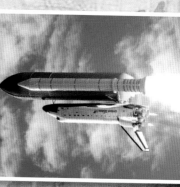

Space Shuttle
Atlantis blasts off from Kennedy Space Center, Florida in 2011.

## NEW TECHNOLOGY

The USA is a world leader in science, technology and manufacturing. In the 1920s businessman Henry Ford pioneered the first fast production line, which mass-produced motor cars. In the late 1900s the US space agency NASA landed men on the Moon and pioneered a reusable spacecraft, the Space Shuttle. The area known as 'Silicon Valley' in California is an important centre for electronics and computers.

Popular TV and film characters such as "Alvin and The Chipmunks" are created in the USA.

## PEOPLE

The USA has one of the world's most varied populations. The population mix includes Native Americans (the country's original inhabitants), Europeans who have migrated to the USA since the 1600s, and African Americans, some of whom are descended from African slaves. There are also many people of Mexican descent living in America, and people from all over the world continue to settle here. The USA has been called a nation of immigrants.

## FILMS AND MUSIC

The film industry in the USA is one of the world's oldest and American TV programmes are popular all over the globe. Hollywood, where film companies such as Walt Disney are based, is the famous centre of the film industry. American music, such as jazz, blues and hip hop, is also enjoyed by people worldwide.

An American crowd at a sports game.

## HISTORY ZONE
### New York City

New York is the largest city in the USA in terms of population, followed by Los Angeles and Chicago. New York grew up around a natural harbour at the mouth of the Hudson river. In the 1800s and 1900s, tens of thousands of immigrants – people moving from other countries in search of a better life – came to the city. Now dominated by skyscrapers, New York is a leading centre for business, finance, trade and the arts. Over eight million people live here.

New York City was one of the first cities to build tall skyscrapers.

# THE AMERICAS

The awesome Americas stretch from Greenland in the far north to Cape Horn in the south, making up nearly 30 per cent of Earth's dry land. Earth's third-largest continent, North America, is linked to South America, the fourth-largest, by the narrow neck of land that is Central America. There is an amazing range of habitats in the Americas – polar conditions in the far north, and vast rolling grasslands, large lakes and deserts further south. The Americas also include some of the world's greatest mountain ranges, mighty rivers and our planet's largest rainforest, the Amazon.

## NORTH AMERICA FACT FILE

**HIGHEST PEAK:**
Denali, Alaska: 6,168 m

**LONGEST RIVER:**
Mississippi-Missouri: 6,019 km

**LARGEST LAKE:**
Superior: 82,103 sq km

**HIGHEST WATERFALL:**
Yosemite Falls, California: 739 m

**LARGEST DESERT:**
The Chihuahuan Desert, US / Mexico border: 362,600 sq km

## NATURAL WONDERS

## MAJESTIC MOUNTAINS

The snow-capped Rocky Mountains run for 4,800 km in North America, parallel to the west coast. In South America, the towering Andes are the world's longest mountain chain, forming a backbone that runs for 7,250 km. Many of the highest peaks in the Andes are volcanoes.

## GRAND CANYON

The stunning Grand Canyon in western USA is one of the world's best-known natural wonders. This vast canyon is up to 1.8 km deep and 29 km wide and stretches for over 440 km. It formed over millions of years as the Colorado River carved its way through solid rock, forming a high plateau.

The Grand Canyon.

# NORTH AMERICA

ARCTIC OCEAN

ATLANTIC OCEAN

PACIFIC OCEAN

*Niagara Falls – three huge waterfalls, the most powerful in North America.

*Old Faithful, Yellowstone National Park – a giant geyser that shoots boiling water about 50 m into the air.

The dramatic peaks and lakes of the Rocky Mountains.

Polar bear

Arctic Circle

Arctic fox

Resolute

HUDSON BAY

Moose

Beaver

Washington D.C.

Niagara Falls

Everglades

Hurricane

Lake Superior

GREAT LAKES

Mississippi river

Great Plains

Missouri river

Rattlesnake

Rio Grande

Chihuah

Grand Canyon

Death Valley

Bison

Old Faithful

Grizzly bear

Mackenzie river

Rocky Mountains

Yosemite Falls

Denali

GULF OF ALASKA

Narwhal

Great White shark

N
E
S
W

## MUST SEE!

☑ The ROYAL CANADIAN MOUNTED POLICE, or Mounties, are famous for their red jackets and broad-brimmed hats.

☑ The CN TOWER in Toronto is the third tallest tower in the world, rising 553 m above the city.

## FISHING

The Grand Banks off the east coast of Canada were once one of the world's best fishing grounds. Fishing fleets came from far away to catch cod here. However intensive fishing caused cod numbers to drop steeply, and the industry collapsed in the 1990s. Salmon fishing is still important in Canada. Fish stocks are checked to make sure enough fish are left in the waters.

Salmon farming.

A freight ship on the St Lawrence Seaway.

## RIVER TRANSPORT

Canada's many rivers and lakes were once used to explore this vast country. They are still vital for transport. The Great Lakes on the US border form a watery highway that connects to the St Lawrence Seaway and the Atlantic. Ocean-going ships can travel all the way to the western tip of Lake Superior, a distance of 3,769 km.

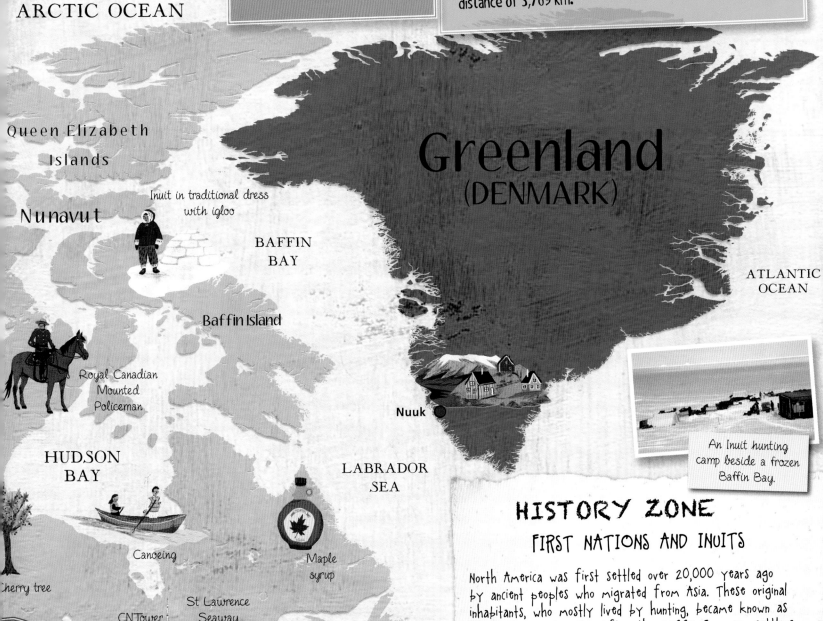

ARCTIC OCEAN

Queen Elizabeth Islands

Nunavut

Inuit in traditional dress with igloo

BAFFIN BAY

Baffin Island

Greenland
(DENMARK)

ATLANTIC OCEAN

Nuuk

Royal Canadian Mounted Policeman

HUDSON BAY

An Inuit hunting camp beside a frozen Baffin Bay.

LABRADOR SEA

Canoeing

Cherry tree

Maple syrup

St Lawrence Seaway

CN Tower

Lake Superior
GREAT LAKES
Lake Michigan
Lake Huron
Toronto
Lake Erie
Lake Ontario
Ottawa
Montreal

Fishing boat

GRAND BANKS

## HISTORY ZONE
### FIRST NATIONS AND INUITS

North America was first settled over 20,000 years ago by ancient peoples who migrated from Asia. These original inhabitants, who mostly lived by hunting, became known as First Nations and Inuits. After the 1600s, European settlers seized the lands of the First Nations. In 1999 a vast homeland was awarded to the Inuit in northeastern Canada. It is called Nunavut, which means 'our land'.

# MEGA CITY

The Mexican capital, Mexico City, is one of the world's largest cities, with over 20 million people. The city stands on the soft soil of a dried-up lake. In 1985, an earthquake turned the soft ground to mud, and many buildings collapsed. The city has now been rebuilt. Nearby is a tall, active volcano called Popocatépetl.

Mexico City is ringed by mountains.

# PANAMA CANAL

The Panama Canal cuts right across Panama, linking the Atlantic and Pacific Oceans. This 77-km waterway saves ships from making a 15,000-km journey around the tip of South America. The canal was completed in 1914 and is now a key shipping route.

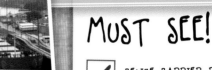
Ships at a lock on the Panama canal.

## MUST SEE!

☑ BELIZE BARRIER REEF is the world's second-longest coral reef, running for 300 km offshore. The reef has spectacular marine life.

☑ GRAY WHALES swim all the way from the Arctic to give birth in the warm waters of the Gulf of California. You can see these huge mammals and their babies from the shore or from a boat.

☑ The Mayan city of TIKAL in Guatemala has a pyramid temple 47 m high.

Corn tortillas

Rio Grande

MEXICO

Mariachi band

Gray whale

Marias Islands

GULF OF CALIFORNIA

Aztec headdress

Chicle tapper

GULF OF MEXICO

PACIFIC OCEAN

Rio Grande de Santiago

Mexico City

Mt Popocatépetl

Pyramid at Tikal

Belmop

GUATEMAL

Guatemala City

EL SALVADOR

San Salvado

# PLANTATIONS

Crops grow well in the warm tropical climate of this region. Sugar cane, tobacco, coffee, cotton and bananas are grown on plantations and sold abroad. These plantations were once worked by slaves from Africa. Local farmers also grow potatoes, rice and maize to feed their families. Chewing gum is made from sap called chicle, produced by a local tree.

Transporting sugar cane on the Caribbean island of St Kitts.

# DAY OF THE DEAD

A festival called the Day of the Dead is held in Mexico each November to remember loved ones who have died. People believe the souls of the dead return to visit friends and relatives on this day. Special foods are prepared, including sweets in the shape of skulls. Offerings of flowers and candles are placed on graves.

Colourful Day of the Dead ornamental skulls.

# SOUTH AMERICA

CARIBBEAN SEA

CENTRAL AMERICA

Equator

Amazon Rainforest

Angel Falls

Amazon

Jaguar

Anteater

Amazon river

Anaconda

Parrot

Monkey

Andes Mountains

Iguazu Falls

Paraná river

Rhea

Buenos Aires

ATLANTIC OCEAN

Patagonian desert

Rockhopper penguin

Cape Horn

Monarch butterfly

Galapagos tortoise

Marine iguana

GALAPAGOS ISLANDS

Lake Titicaca

Atacama Desert

Mt Aconcagua

PACIFIC OCEAN

Torres del Paine

## Legend

 Areas of high ground — Tropical rainforest

 Major mountain ranges — Mild climate with plants such as deciduous trees

 Grassland areas with hot summers and cold winters — Tropical grassland

 Cold climate with plants such as evergreen trees — Desert

 Very cold climate with mosses and small shrubs — Bitterly cold climate with snow and ice

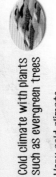

## WEATHER REPORT

**Average temperature and rainfall figures:**

* Resolute, Canada
  Jan: -30 °C    Jan: 4.2 mm
  July: 7 °C     July: 28 mm

* Washington D.C., USA
  Jan: 6 °C      Jan: 71 mm
  July: 31 °C    July: 94 mm

* Buenos Aires, Argentina
  Jan: 25 °C     Jan: 93 mm
  July: 11 °C    July: 56 mm

## RECORDS

Death Valley, California USA - as hot as 56.7 °C!

Atacama desert - some areas have average rainfall of 0 mm!

The Amazon river runs through dense rainforest.

# HOTSPOTS!

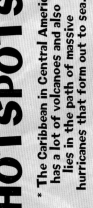  

* The Caribbean in Central America has a lot of volcanoes and also lies in the path of massive hurricanes that form out to sea.

* The west coast of the USA is prone to earthquakes.

* Several tornadoes a year hit 'Tornado Alley' - an area in the grasslands of central USA.

## ATACAMA DESERT

The Atacama Desert along the west coast of South America is Earth's driest place. In some parts of this barren region no rain at all has fallen for centuries – ever since records began.

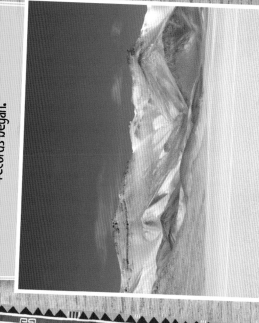

The Atacama Desert near the border of Chile and Bolivia.

## AMAZON RIVER AND RAINFOREST

At at least 6,400 km long, the Amazon River is the world's second longest river. It contains more water than the five next-biggest rivers combined. On its way from the Andes Mountains to the Atlantic Ocean, the river winds through the lush Amazon rainforest. Nowhere on Earth has as many different types of plants and animals, and new species are being found all the time.

## WILDLIFE WATCH

The mountains, forests, lakes, rivers, deserts and islands of the Americas are home to a huge variety of wildlife. Parrots, toucans and over 1,500 types of birds live in the Amazon rainforest. There are also frogs, reptiles, mammals such as monkeys and well over two million types of insect. The Galapagos Islands are home to animals found nowhere else, such as marine iguanas.

# FACT FILE

**HIGHEST PEAK:**
Mt Aconcagua: 6,961 m

**LONGEST RIVER:**
Amazon: 6,400 km

**LARGEST LAKE:**
Titicaca: 8,372 sq km

**HIGHEST WATERFALL:**
Angel Falls, Venezuela: 979 m, the highest in the world

**LARGEST DESERT:**
Patagonian Desert: 673,000 sq km

## NATURAL WONDER

*Torres del Paine - an area of dramatic mountains, cliffs and glaciers.

Toucans inhabit the Amazon rainforest.

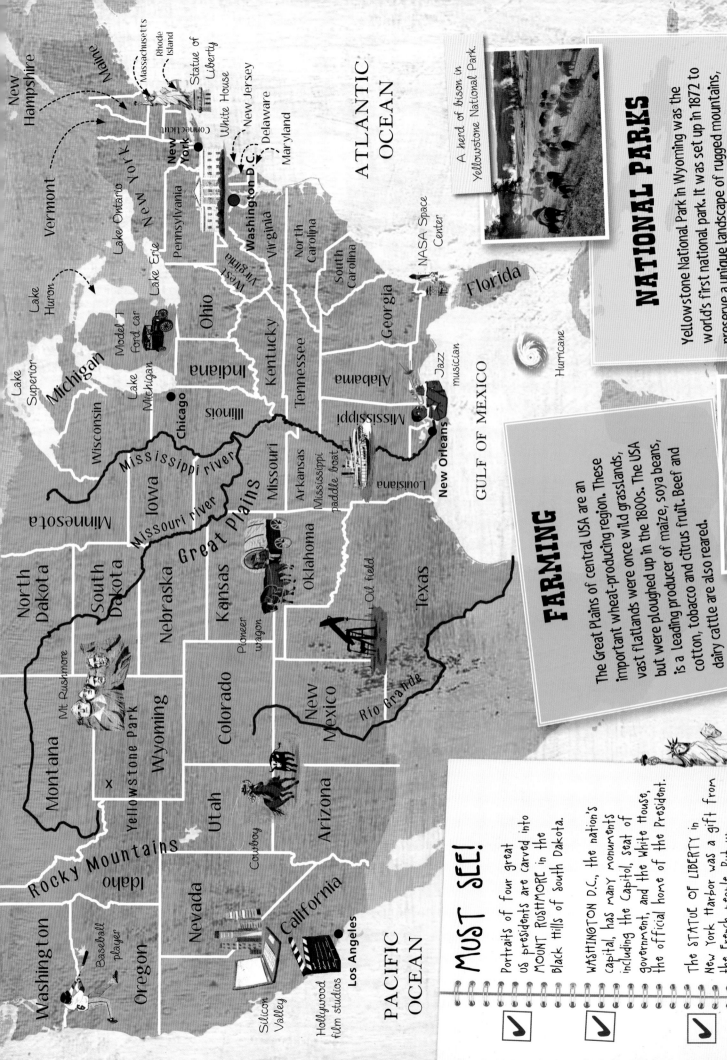

New Hampshire
Maine
Massachusetts
Rhode Island
Statue of Liberty
White House
New Jersey
Delaware
Maryland
Connecticut
**New York**
Vermont
New York
Lake Ontario
Lake Erie
Pennsylvania
**Washington D.C.**
Virginia
West Virginia
North Carolina
South Carolina
Georgia
Florida
NASA Space Center
Lake Huron
Model T ford car
Michigan
Ohio
Indiana
Kentucky
Tennessee
Alabama
Jazz musician
Lake Superior
Lake Michigan
Wisconsin
Chicago
Illinois
Mississippi
Mississippi river
Missouri
Arkansas
Mississippi paddle boat
Louisiana
**New Orleans**
GULF OF MEXICO
Hurricane
Minnesota
Iowa
Missouri river
Great Plains
Oklahoma
Oil field
Texas
Pioneer wagon
North Dakota
South Dakota
Nebraska
Kansas
Colorado
New Mexico
Rio Grande
Mt Rushmore
Yellowstone Park
Wyoming
Montana
x
Rocky Mountains
Idaho
Utah
Arizona
Cowboy
Washington
Oregon
Nevada
California
Baseball player
Silicon Valley
Hollywood film studios
**Los Angeles**
PACIFIC OCEAN
ATLANTIC OCEAN

# NATIONAL PARKS

A herd of bison in Yellowstone National Park.

Yellowstone National Park in Wyoming was the world's first national park. It was set up in 1872 to preserve a unique landscape of rugged mountains, forests, lakes and hot springs. The USA now has over 59 national parks, including the Grand Canyon and Yosemite in California and the Everglades in Florida.

# FARMING

The Great Plains of central USA are an important wheat-producing region. These vast flatlands were once wild grasslands, but were ploughed up in the 1800s. The USA is a leading producer of maize, soya beans, cotton, tobacco and citrus fruit. Beef and dairy cattle are also reared.

Combine harvesters at work in a wheat field in Kansas, USA.

# MUST SEE!

✓ Portraits of four great US presidents are carved into MOUNT RUSHMORE in the Black Hills of South Dakota.

✓ WASHINGTON D.C., the nation's capital, has many monuments including the Capitol, seat of government, and the White House, the official home of the President.

✓ The STATUE OF LIBERTY in New York harbor was a gift from the French people. Put up in 1886 it stands 93 m high.

# Mexico, the Caribbean and Central America

The narrow bridge of land that joins North and South America is called Central America and includes small countries such as Belize and Costa Rica. Mexico lies to the north. Mexico and Central America have mountains, high plateaus, rainforests and deserts. Off the east coast are the islands of the Caribbean, which are made up of about 30 territories, 13 of which are independent countries. From the 1500s to the 1800s, this area was ruled by European powers such as Spain, France and the United Kingdom, but almost all countries are now independent. The region has mineral riches and fertile farmland, but is regularly struck by earthquakes, volcanic eruptions and hurricanes.

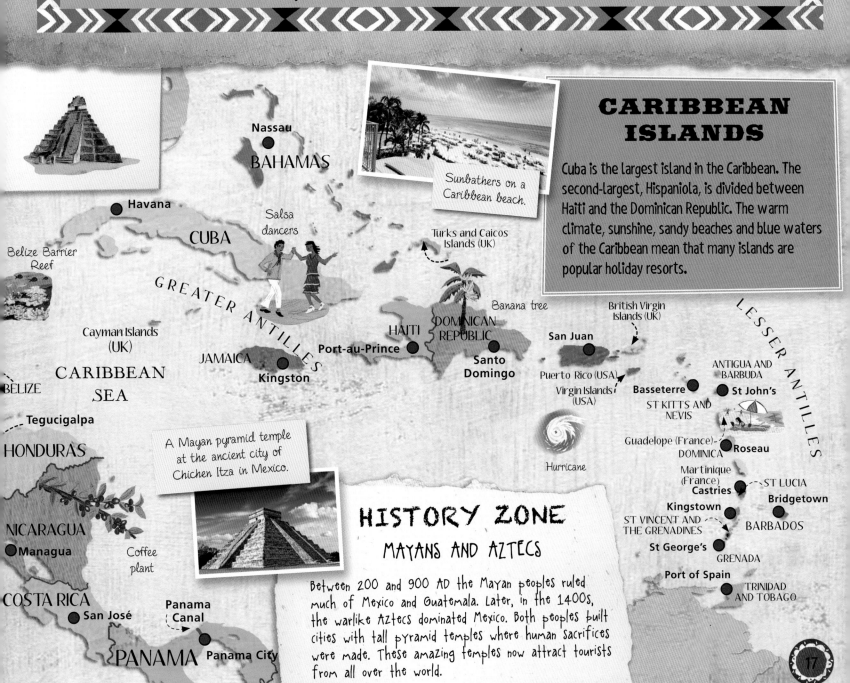

Sunbathers on a Caribbean beach.

Nassau
BAHAMAS

Havana

Salsa dancers

CUBA

Belize Barrier Reef

GREATER ANTILLES

Turks and Caicos Islands (UK)

Banana tree

Cayman Islands (UK)

JAMAICA

Kingston

HAITI
Port-au-Prince

DOMINICAN REPUBLIC
Santo Domingo

San Juan

British Virgin Islands (UK)

LESSER ANTILLES

BELIZE

CARIBBEAN SEA

Puerto Rico (USA)
Virgin Islands (USA)

Basseterre

ANTIGUA AND BARBUDA
St John's

ST KITTS AND NEVIS

Tegucigalpa

A Mayan pyramid temple at the ancient city of Chichen Itza in Mexico.

HONDURAS

Guadelope (France)
DOMINICA
Roseau

Hurricane

Martinique (France)
Castries

ST LUCIA

Bridgetown

Kingstown
ST VINCENT AND THE GRENADINES

BARBADOS

NICARAGUA

Managua

Coffee plant

St George's

GRENADA

Port of Spain

TRINIDAD AND TOBAGO

COSTA RICA

San José

Panama Canal

PANAMA
Panama City

## CARIBBEAN ISLANDS

Cuba is the largest island in the Caribbean. The second-largest, Hispaniola, is divided between Haiti and the Dominican Republic. The warm climate, sunshine, sandy beaches and blue waters of the Caribbean mean that many islands are popular holiday resorts.

## HISTORY ZONE
### MAYANS AND AZTECS

Between 200 and 900 AD the Mayan peoples ruled much of Mexico and Guatemala. Later, in the 1400s, the warlike Aztecs dominated Mexico. Both peoples built cities with tall pyramid temples where human sacrifices were made. These amazing temples now attract tourists from all over the world.

17

# SOUTH AMERICA

The continent of South America is almost entirely surrounded by sea. It's made up of 12 countries of which Brazil is the largest, with half the continent's population. From the 1500s to 1800s all of South America was ruled by Spain, Portugal and other European countries, but now almost all of the former colonies are independent. This region is called Latin America because the Latin-based languages of Spanish and Portuguese are spoken here. As well as having the world's largest rainforest, South America also has the world's largest wetland, the world's driest desert and vast grasslands. The region has a rich and varied culture.

A dragon float in procession at the Rio Carnival.

## RIO CARNIVAL

The five days before Lent, which leads up to the Christian festival of Easter, are carnival time in the Brazilian city of Rio de Janeiro. In this world-famous festival, people take to the streets in amazing costumes. There are parades with floats, and dancing to live music. Many people celebrate until dawn.

VENEZUELA

Caracas

COLOMBIA

Bogotá

Emeralds

ECUADOR

Quito

PERU

Lima

Machu Picchu

Quechua people

Banana tree

Reed boat on lake

GUYANA

Georgetown

Sugar cane

Paramaribo

SURINAME

Cayenne

French Guiana (FRANCE)

AMAZON RAINFOREST

Amazon river

Amazon tribespeople

BRAZIL

Famous footballer Pelé

Brazil nut trees

Brasília cathedral and bell tower

PACIFIC OCEAN

Fishing boat

Christ the
Redeemer statue
**Rio de Janeiro** ●

## MUST SEE!

✔ LAKE TITICACA between Peru and Bolivia is the world's highest lake on which large boats can sail. It lies 3,810 m above sea level.

✔ The statue of CHRIST THE REDEEMER overlooks the beautiful city of Rio de Janeiro. It stands 30 m tall.

✔ In 1960 Brazil moved its capital to the new city of BRASILIA, which was built near the centre of the country. This modern city is laid out in the shape of a plane.

## MINERAL WEALTH

South America's mineral wealth includes oil in the north, particularly in Venezuela. Copper and iron ore are mined further south. It was the promise of gold and silver that brought the Spanish to South America. They seized the golden treasure of the Incas. They also searched for a fabled golden city called El Dorado, 'the golden one', but never found it.

An oil rig off the coast of Venezuela.

## CASSAVA AND CATTLE

Coffee, sugar cane, rubber, soya beans, cocoa and bananas are grown for export. Crops such as potatoes, tomatoes and cassava originally came from South America and are now grown in many parts of the world. Cattle are ranched on grasslands such as the Pampas in Argentina. Beef, milk and hides from Argentina are sold abroad.

Gaucho cowboys herd cattle on the Pampas.

Paraguayan harp

Coffee plant

**PARAGUAY**

**Asunción** ●

Paraná river

**URUGUAY**

**Montevideo** ●

**ARGENTINA**

**Buenos Aires** ●

**PAMPAS**

Gaucho cowboy

Steelworks

**CHILE**

S

**Santiago** ●

Wine

Falkland Islands (Islas Malvinas) (UK)

# ATLANTIC OCEAN

Cave of Hands (A cave with hand paintings that are thousands of years old!)

# HISTORY ZONE
## INCA STRONGHOLD

In the 1400s and 1500s AD the Inca peoples of Peru ruled over a large empire which also included parts of Ecuador, Colombia, Bolivia, Argentina and Chile. Paved roads linked distant parts of the empire. Spanish soldiers conquered the Incas in the 1530s, but never found this amazing ruined city in the mountains is a busy tourist attraction.

The Incas crafted beautiful objects, such as this gold ceremonial mask.

A couple dancing a tango in Buenos Aires.

## THE TANGO

A dance called the tango began in the poor districts of Buenos Aires in Argentina and Montevideo in Uruguay in the late 1800s. This dramatic dance, performed to stirring music, is now popular all over the world.

## RANCHING

Australia and New Zealand are famous for sheep and cattle ranching. In Australia, the largest cattle stations (ranches) cover thousands of square kilometres. Cattle are often rounded up by helicopter. Beef, lamb, wool, hides and milk are important exports of the region. Most of Australia is too dry for farming, but wheat, sugar cane and grapes are grown in wetter areas. Fruits such as apples, oranges and kiwi fruit are produced in New Zealand.

A beef cattle ranch in Australia.

## AMAZING WILDLIFE

Australia's best-known animals, such as kangaroos and koalas, are marsupials. The babies are born when they are still very tiny, and grow up in their mothers' pouches. The world's only egg-laying mammals, the platypus and echidna, also live in Australia. New Zealand has very unusual wildlife, including kiwis, penguins and a parrot that cannot fly.

Kangaroos live in the open grasslands of Australia.

## MUST SEE!

☑ The GREAT BARRIER REEF runs for 2,600 km off the east coast of Australia. The reef is home to tropical fish, sponges, starfish and turtles.

☑ ULURU, or Ayers Rock, is a huge sandstone outcrop rising from a flat desert. The site is sacred to Aboriginals.

☑ SYDNEY OPERA HOUSE opened in the 1970s. Its curving roofs resemble sails.

INDIAN OCEAN

Boomerang

Sheep shearing

Aboriginal with didgeridoo

# AUSTRALIA

Kookaburra

● Perth

Uluru (Ayers Rock)

Lake Eyre (Kati Thand

Great Victoria Desert

Opal mine

Great White Shark

Tourists enjoy bungee jumping in Australia and New Zealand.

### LANDSCAPE KEY

Areas of high ground

Milder climate with plants such as decideous trees

Mountains

Hot, dry grassland

Tropical rainforest

Desert

## SPORT

Outdoor sports of all kinds are popular in Australia and New Zealand. Australians love surfing, swimming and sailing. New Zealanders are keen on hiking and white-water rafting. Commercial bungee jumping began in New Zealand in 1986. Both countries also have world-class cricket and rugby teams.

# AUSTRALIA AND NEW ZEALAND

PAPUA NEW GUINEA

Oceania is the world's smallest continent and sixth-largest country. It has a hot climate and most inland areas are desert or dry scrubland, known as the Outback. Many of the country's 22 million people live on the coast, in cities such as Sydney, Melbourne and Perth. Australia is rich in minerals and is known for its unique wildlife. New Zealand, 2,000 km to the east, has dramatic scenery, including snowy peaks, volcanoes and fjords (deep, coastal inlets). Australia, New Zealand and the South Pacific islands form a region called Oceania (see p. 55).

Great Barrier Reef

Koala

Darling river

Brisbane

Redback spider

Sydney

Sydney Opera House

Canberra

ray river

Mt Kosciuszko

Melbourne

platypus Tasmania

Hobart

A collapsed house in the Christchurch earthquake of 2011.

## AUSTRALIA & NEW ZEALAND FACT FILE

**HIGHEST PEAKS:**
Mt Kosciuszko, Australia: 2,229 m

Mt Cook, New Zealand: 3,754 m

**LONGEST RIVER:**
Murray-Darling, Australia: 3,750 km

**LARGEST DESERT:**
Great Victoria Desert, Australia: 348,750 sq km

TASMAN SEA

## VOLCANIC NEW ZEALAND

New Zealand lies on a deep crack in Earth's crust called a faultline. Volcanoes and earthquakes are common along these cracks. In 2011 a major earthquake shook the city of Christchurch. New Zealand has many volcanoes, some of which are active. The country's largest lake lies in the crater of an extinct volcano. At Rotorua, volcanic activity produces pools of bubbling mud and geysers which spout hot water.

## HISTORY ZONE
### First Inhabitants

Australia's first inhabitants were Aboriginals, who may have migrated from South Asia or Africa more than 40,000 years ago. In 1770 English explorer James Cook claimed Australia for Britain. It was first used as a prison colony. In the 1800s and 1900s, large numbers of Europeans and also Asians moved to Australia. About 700 years ago, New Zealand was colonized by a Polynesian people called the Maori. Europeans arrived in the 1800s.

The Maori were the first inhabitants of New Zealand.

Kiwi

North Island

Rotorua mud pools

NEW ZEALAND

Wellington

Southern Alps

Mt Cook (Aoraki)

South Island

PACIFIC OCEAN

Maori in traditional dress

# HISTORY ZONE
## VOLCANIC ERUPTIONS

Many small islands in Southeast Asia are the tips of volcanoes rising from the sea bed. Some of them are active. In 1991 Mount Pinatubo on Luzon in the Philippines erupted, covering nearby towns and villages with a thick layer of ash. In 1883 the volcanic island of Krakatoa in Indonesia exploded with an enormous bang which could be heard more than 3,200 km away.

A plume of gas and ash erupts from Mount Pinatubo in 1991.

Rubies

Banana carrier

Irrawaddy river

BURMA (MYANMAR)

Nay Pyi Taw

LAOS

Hanoi

Vientiane

Buddha

Rangoon

Rice growing

THAILAND

Mekong river

VIETNAM

Bangkok

Angkor Wat

CAMBODIA

Phnom Penh

Floating market

Tourists on a beach

Luzon

Mt Pinatubo

Manila

PHILIPPINES

Fishing boat

Petronas Towers

Bandar Seri Begawan

MALAYSIA BRUNEI

Sultan of Brunei's palace

The modern skyline of Singapore.

Kuala Lumpur

Putrajaya

Singapore

Freight ship

Sumatra

SINGAPORE

Borneo

Coconut palm

Celebes

## SINGAPORE

The tiny island state of Singapore is a centre for high-tech industries. The biggest port in the region, Singapore is also known for repairing ships, refining oil and finance. This small country has very strict laws. For example, it is against the law to drop litter or chew gum.

INDONESIA

Jakarta

Indonesian fishing boat

Mt Krakatoa

Borobudur temples

Java

Dili

EA TIM

# SOUTHEAST ASIA

Southeast Asia stretches in a great arc from Burma to Indonesia and New Guinea. This region has high mountains cut by river valleys that form swampy deltas near the coast. Southeast Asia includes thousands of islands, which form nations such as Indonesia and the Philippines. Some islands have few people, but Java and Singapore are densely populated. Farming and mining have been important for centuries, but in recent years forestry and high-tech industries have grown. Dense rainforest once covered much of the region, but now forests are disappearing fast as they are cut down for timber or to make way for farmland.

e field terraces
t into the hills
in Vietnam.

## RICE AND RUBBER

ce is the most important crop of
outheast Asia. The hot, wet climate is
eal for rice-growing. Steep hillsides
re cut into flat terraces to make small
ields that can be flooded with water to
row rice. Sugar cane, bananas, rubber and
il palms are grown on large plantations.

Statues of the Buddha, whose teachings form the basis of Buddhism, are seen in many parts of Southeast Asia.

## MANY FAITHS

Buddhism is the main religion on most of the mainland of Southeast Asia. Buddhism arrived from India in the 1st centuries AD. Islam is the main faith of most island nations, including Indonesia. However in the Philippines, many people are Christians.

## WILDLIFE TOURISM

Southeast Asian wildlife includes some spectacular animals that are a draw for tourists. Orangutans are large apes that live in the rainforests of Borneo and Sumatra. They are put at risk when people cut down these forests, destroying their homes. The Sumatran rhino inhabits the forests of Sumatra and is also very rare.

Tourists visit a care centre for orangutans that have been orphaned due to destruction of forests or hunting.

PACIFIC
OCEAN

New Guinea

Turtle

Tribesman

## MUST SEE!

The Buddhist temples of BOROBUDUR on the island of Java date from the 9th century AD. The site has over 500 statues of the Buddha. ✔

Bangkok, capital of Thailand, was built on an island in a river and has many canals. Farmers sell their produce from small boats called 'sampans', which form FLOATING MARKETS. ✔

The PETRONAS TOWERS, in the Malaysian capital Kuala Lumpur, are the tallest twin towers in the world, at about 452 m high. ✔

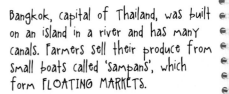

# EAST ASIA

The eastern reaches of Asia are home to some of the world's oldest civilizations. The region has many different cultures, and hundreds of languages are spoken here. To the east lie the islands of Japan and Taiwan, and the Korean Peninsula, which is divided into North and South Korea. The plains and deserts of Mongolia lie to the north. Few people live in the dry and mountainous parts of East Asia, while the river valleys and coasts are densely populated. China is the world's most populated country, with over 1.3 billion people.

## MUST SEE!

☑ The THREE GORGES DAM on the Yangtze River in China is the most powerful dam in the world and was finished in 2012. It supplies electri to nearby Chinese cities.

☑ The historic Japanese city of K has many beautiful temples.

☑ The GREAT WALL OF CHINA built over 2,000 years ago. It runs for about 6,400 km!

Coal mine

## BOOM CITIES

Some of the world's largest cities are found in East Asia, including Shanghai and Beijing in China, Tokyo in Japan and Seoul in South Korea. The Chinese port of Shanghai has grown very quickly. High-rise buildings, motorways and flyovers have transformed the city in the last 20 years.

Tokyo, Japan, is a fast-moving city.

Chinese food

Chinese calligraphy

Confucius

Potala pala

A big electronics factory in China.

## BUSY FACTORIES

Cars, computers, cameras, TVs and other electronic goods are made in East Asia in large numbers. Manufacturing has grown and developed here in the last years. In the 1950s, Japan began to modernize its industries, followed by Taiwan, South Korea and more recently, China. China is now the world's second-biggest economy, after the USA.

HIMALAYAS

## HISTORY ZONE
### CHINESE RULERS

From 221 BC to 1912 AD China was ruled by emperors. The title of emperor was handed down from father to son, and Chinese history is divided into ruling families called dynasties. In 1949 the Communists under Chairman Mao took control of China. In recent years, China's Communist leaders have opened the country to world trade.

Chairman Mao.

INDIAN OCEAN

## HEALTHY DIET

Fish and rice are the most important foods of Japan. This healthy diet means that Japanese people generally live a long time. Japan has one of the world's largest fishing fleets. Sushi are rice patties topped with raw fish, vegetables or seaweed. China is the world's number one producer of rice.

Sushi.

## CHINESE TRADITIONS

The Chinese dragon dance is performed at New Year to bring good luck. Civilization began in China at least 5,000 years ago. Taoism and Confucianism are ancient Chinese beliefs. The philosopher Confucius, who lived around 500 BC, taught the importance of family loyalties and honouring ancestors. The Buddhist religion arrived from India almost 2,000 years ago.

Chinese dragon dancers.

Mongol herdsman

**Ulan Bator** ●

Herdsman's yurt

MONGOLIA

OBI DESERT

Cyclist

Dragon dance

Fast 'Bullet' train

The Great Wall of China

NORTH KOREA

SEA OF JAPAN

CHINA

**Beijing**

Forbidden City, once home to the emperors

Pyongyang

JAPAN

Kyoto Palace

**Tokyo**

Computer

Seoul

SOUTH KOREA

Yellow river

Terracotta army, built by China's first emperor

Shanghai skyline

Mt Fuji

Yangtze river

X

Three Gorges Dam

Rice terrace

Chinese junk

Sushi

PACIFIC OCEAN

## MARTIAL ARTS

East Asia is the home of martial arts such as karate, judo and kung fu. The Japanese sport of kendo is the art of fighting with bamboo swords. Sumo wrestling is a national sport in Japan. Sumo wrestlers eat a special diet to put on weight.

Toy factory

Taipei 101 building

**Taipei** ●

**Hong Kong** ●

TAIWAN

Hainan

SOUTH CHINA SEA

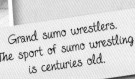

Grand sumo wrestlers. The sport of sumo wrestling is centuries old.

25

# WILDLIFE WATCH

An incredible range of wildlife lives in the mountains, forests, deserts, plains and islands of Asia. Snow leopards and large, hairy cattle called yaks live in the high Himalayas. Tigers, elephants, rhinos and orangutans are found in tropical forests. The rare giant panda lives in the bamboo forests of China. The Indonesian island of Komodo is home to the world's largest lizard, the Komodo dragon.

The giant panda has been widely hunted and is now rare.

Ural Mountains

Ob river

Yenisey River

Altai Mou.

BLACK SEA

Aral Sea

CASPIAN SEA

Taklamakan Desert

Snow leopard

Karakoram Mountains

Yak

Plateau of

Mt.

Damascus

Tigris river

DEAD SEA

Euphrates river

Arabian Peninsula

Indus river

Himalayas

Ganges river

Mawsynram

Indian

RED SEA

Arabian oryx

ARABIAN SEA

Dudhsagar Falls

Irrawad river

Butterfly Fi

Equator

## LANDSCAPE KEY

Areas of high ground

Cold climate with plants such as evergreen trees

Tropical grassland

Major mountain ranges

Tropical rainforest

Grassland areas with hot summers and cold winters

Mild climate with plants such as deciduous trees

Desert

Very cold climate with mosses and small shrubs

INDIAN OCEAN

# ASIA

Amazing Asia is Earth's largest continent. It is made up of nearly a third of all Earth's dry land and well over half of the world's population. It includes some of the world's largest and also most densely populated countries. Asia stretches from the Arctic to the Equator, and from the Arabian Peninsula in the west all the way to Japan and Southeast Asia. This vast continent has a huge range of landscapes including towering mountains, windswept plains and stony or sandy deserts. There are huge conifer forests in the north, tropical forests in the south, fertile river valleys and countless islands, large and small.

## MOUNTAIN RANGES

The world's ten highest peaks all lie in Asia, in the Himalayas and nearby Karakoram mountains. Both these mountain ranges were formed more recently than those elsewhere in the world – about 70 million years ago – and they are still getting taller! North of the Himalayas, there is a remote high plain called the Tibetan Plateau, also known as the 'Roof of the World'.

The icy peaks of Dorje Lhakpa mountain in the Himalayas.

Boggy tundra landscape.

Sunset over the Ganges river in India.

## FROZEN LAND

Barren, treeless plains cover Siberia in northern Russia. These lands are called the tundra. Mosses and small shrubs grow here. The ground is frozen and snow-covered for much of the year. In summer, the snow and top layer of soil melts, and the area turns to bog.

## GREAT RIVERS

Many of Asia's great rivers rise in the mountains of the west and flow thousands of kilometres to the sea. China's greatest rivers are the Yangtze and Yellow rivers. The Ganges river in India is sacred. Huge swampy areas called deltas form where rivers meet the sea. The Ganges Delta is the world's largest delta.

# SOUTH ASIA

Most of South Asia is a huge peninsula jutting out into the ocean. This region is called the Indian subcontinent, and is separated from the rest of Asia by the snow-capped Himalayas. More than one-fifth of the world's people live in South Asia. India is the world's seventh-biggest country, and has the second-largest population after China, with about 1.2 billion people. As well as towering mountains, South Asia has forests, grasslands and deserts. Traditionally farming has been the main occupation and most people live in the countryside, but now industries and cities are growing very fast.

## RELIGIONS

Hinduism began in India more than 4,500 years ago. It is the world's oldest living religion and has many gods and goddesses. Buddhism has no gods. It was founded in the 6th century BC by an Indian prince called Siddhartha, also known as the Buddha. It later spread eastwards across Asia. Today India and Nepal are mostly Hindu; Sri Lanka and Bhutan are mainly Buddhist, and Pakistan, Bangladesh and Afghanistan are mainly Muslim.

A colourful Hindu temple in India.

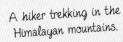
A hiker trekking in the Himalayan mountains.

## BOLLYWOOD!

The film industry based in Mumbai (Bombay) in western India is known as Bollywood – a shortening of 'Bombay Hollywood'. These films are known for their glamorous stars and spectacular dance and fight scenes. Over 800 films are produced in India each year, more than in the whole of the USA.

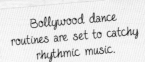
Bollywood dance routines are set to catchy rhythmic music.

## HOLIDAY SPOTS

Mount Everest, in the Himalayas, was first climbed in 1953. This highest of the world's mountain ranges remains a magnet for climbers. The historic cities and palaces of India attract millions of sightseers. The palm-fringed beaches, blue waters and coral reefs of the Maldives are perfect for beach holidays.

The coastal city of Mumbai has many high-rise buildings.

## INDUSTRY

India's industries have grown very quickly in the last 30 years. For years, textiles have been a key industry but India is now a leading producer of cars, planes, steel and electronic goods. Cities such as New Dehli and Mumbai are centres for service industries such as banking and insurance.

# MUST SEE!

☑ The TAJ MAHAL in Agra, India, is one of the world's best-known buildings. Built in the 17th century, it has four slender towers called minarets, and a central dome.

☑ Pilgrims flock to VARANASI, India, on the banks of the Ganges river to bathe in the holy river water.

☑ The Buddhist TEMPLE OF THE TOOTH in Kandy on the island of Sri Lanka dates from the 17th century. It houses what is believed to be a tooth of the Buddha.

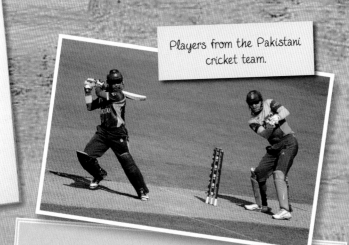
Players from the Pakistani cricket team.

## CRICKET

Many South Asian countries were once part of an empire ruled by the British. They are now independent, but British influence can still be seen in sports such as cricket. India, Pakistan and Sri Lanka all have world-class cricket teams, and you can see the sport being played on open ground throughout the region.

**AFGHANISTAN**
Kabul

Kite

**PAKISTAN**
Islamabad

Sikh temple at Amritsar

Lahore fort

Indus river

Colourful bus

New Delhi

Taj Mahal

Sacred cow

Turtle

**HIMALAYAS**

Mt Everest

**NEPAL**
Kathmandu

Thimphu

**BHUTAN**

Varanasi

Varanasi bathers

Ganges river

**BANGLADESH**
Dhaka

Drummer

Curry

## INDIA

Mumbai

Tea pickers

Clothes factory

## FARMING

The people of Bangladesh are mainly farmers. The main crops grown are rice and jute. This low-lying country is well watered by the Ganges river, but the region is at risk of flooding after heavy monsoon rain and violent storms.

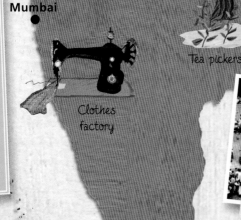
During the partition of India in 1947 many people had to move homes.

## HISTORY ZONE
### PARTITION

India, Pakistan and Bangladesh were once one huge country, much of which was ruled by the British from the mid-1800s. In 1947 the region gained independence, but was 'partitioned' or split into mainly Hindu India and mainly Muslim Pakistan. Following a war between West and East Pakistan in 1971, East Pakistan became an independent country called Bangladesh.

**MALDIVES**

Jute crops are used to make rope.

**SRI LANKA**
Sri Jayewardenepura Kotte
Colombo

Temple of the Tooth

31

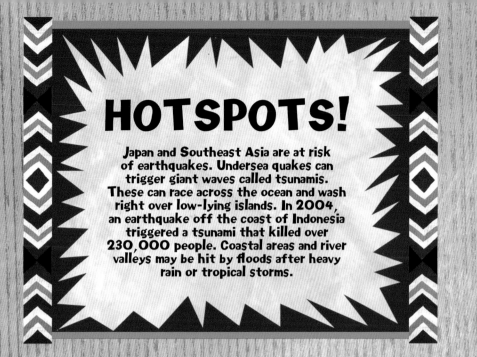

# HOTSPOTS!

Japan and Southeast Asia are at risk of earthquakes. Undersea quakes can trigger giant waves called tsunamis. These can race across the ocean and wash right over low-lying islands. In 2004, an earthquake off the coast of Indonesia triggered a tsunami that killed over 230,000 people. Coastal areas and river valleys may be hit by floods after heavy rain or tropical storms.

## ASIA FACT FILE

**HIGHEST PEAK:**
Mt Everest: 8,848 m

**LOWEST POINT:**
Dead Sea: 423 m below sea level

**LONGEST RIVER:**
Yangtze: 6,380 km

**LARGEST LAKE:**
Caspian Sea: 371,000 sq km

**LARGEST DESERT:**
Gobi Desert: 1.3 million sq km

## DEADLY DESERTS

Asia has vast areas of desert. In the west, much of the Arabian Peninsula is covered by a desert of shifting sands. The Gobi Desert in Mongolia is famous for its dinosaur fossils. The Taklamakan Desert lies in northwest China. Its name means Desert of Death, or 'Go in and you will never get out'.

Unusual rock formations in the Gobi Desert.

A downpour during the monsoon.

## MONSOON RAINS

Southern and eastern Asia are affected by seasonal winds called monsoons. These winds change direction at different times of year, bringing very heavy rain in summer. Farmers rely on the monsoon to grow their crops, but ultra-heavy rain can cause floods.

## NATURAL WONDERS

* Snow-capped volcano Mount Fuji in Japan has been dormant since its last eruption in 1707.

* The Dead Sea in western Asia has one of the world's saltiest bodies of water. The water is so salty it is nearly impossible for a person to sink!

* The soaring limestone peaks of the Guilin Hills in China are a famous beauty spot.

* Dudhsagar Falls in India is a four-tied waterfall. The cascading water looks white like milk.

ARCTIC OCEAN

✳ Verkhoyansk

Arctic Circle

SIBERIA

Lena river

Lake Baikal

Bactrian camel

Gobi Desert

Yellow river

Blue Tiger butterfly

Yangtze river

Guilin Hills

Orangutan

Singapore

Bird of Paradise

Komodo dragon

Octopus

Ust-Kamchatsk

N
W    E
S

PACIFIC OCEAN

SEA OF JAPAN

Mt Fuji

Great White shark

Blue whale

**WEATHER REPORT**
Average temperature and rainfall figures:

✳ Damascus
Jan:   6 °C
July: 27 °C
Jan: 44 mm
July:  0 mm

✳ Ust-Kamchatsk
Jan: -9 °C
July: 13°C
Jan: 85 mm
July: 45 mm

✳ Singapore
Jan: 30 °C
July: 31 °C
Jan: 243 mm
July: 158 mm

**RECORDS**
Coldest place: Verkhoyansk, Siberia: -67.8 °C
Wettest place: Mawsynram, India:
11,872 mm per year

# SOUTHWEST ASIA

Southwest Asia stretches from Syria, Lebanon and Israel on the shores of the Mediterranean eastwards through Iraq to Iran on the Caspian Sea. It also includes the Arabian Peninsula, in which lie Saudi Arabia and many smaller countries. Southwest Asia, sometimes called the Middle East, is the birthplace of three religions: Judaism, Christianity and Islam. More recently, rich reserves of oil and gas were discovered here, which has produced great wealth. However, the region has often been torn by war and conflict, which continues to this day.

## RELIGION AND CONFLICT

Islam, the Muslim faith, began in Arabia in the 7th century AD. Mecca and Medina in Saudi Arabia are holy cities for Muslims. Judaism and Christianity both began in the ancient land of Palestine. In 1948, Israel, the world's only Jewish state, was founded on Palestinian land that had been settled by Arabs for centuries. This has led to conflict between the Jews in Israel and its Arab neighbours.

The Grand Mosque in Mecca is a centre for Muslim pilgrimage.

An oil field in Kuw

## OIL AND GAS

In the early 1900s, oil and natural gas were discovered in the Middle East. These resources have brought great wealth to Iran, Iraq, Saudi Arabia and the many small countries on the Persian Gulf, such as Bahrain, Kuwait and United Arab Emirates (UAE). Saudi Arabia and Iran rank as the world's second and fourth largest oil producers. (Russia and the United States are first and third.)

## ROSE-RED CITY

The ancient city of Petra was built by an Arab people called the Nabateans in the 4th century BC. The tombs and temples here were carved out of solid rose-coloured rock, so Petra is called the 'rose-red city'. Skilled engineers, the Nabateans also carved channels to bring rainwater to this desert city.

The Al Khazneh temple at Petra.

## HISTORY ZONE

### MESOPOTAMIA

About 7,000 years ago, some of the world's oldest civilizations grew up between the Tigris and Euphrates rivers in what is now mainly Iraq. The area was known as Mesopotamia, which means 'land between the rivers'. People began to irrigate the land with river water and became farmers. They built fine cities with stepped pyramids called 'Ziggurats' and invented the earliest form of writing.

## JERUSALEM

Jerusalem, capital of Israel, is sacred to three faiths: Judaism, Christianity and Islam. The Dome of the Rock, a Muslim shrine, stands close to the Western Wall, which marks the site of the Jewish King Solomon's Temple. The Church of the Holy Sepulchre marks the tomb of Jesus Christ.

Jews visit the Western Wall in Jerusalem to pray.

BLACK SEA

GEORGIA
Tbilisi

ARMENIA
Yerevan
AZERBAIJAN
Baku

AZER.

CASPIAN
SEA

TURKEY

Tehran

IRAN

SYRIA

Tigris river

Euphrates river

Beirut
LEBANON
Damascus
Jerusalem
JORDAN
Amman
WEST BANK

IRAQ

Baghdad

Ziggurat of Ur

Woman in
traditional dress

Oil fields

Petra ruins

Mosque

Arabian horse

Kuwait City

KUWAIT

PERSIAN GULF

Persepolis
ruins

Persian carpet

Khalifa Tower

OMAN

SAUDI
ARABIA

Medina

RED
SEA

Riyadh

Ka'bah Muslim
shrine

Mecca

BAHRAIN
Manama
Doha
QATAR

Dubai
Abu Dhabi

UNITED ARAB
EMIRATES

Muscat

OMAN

Bedouins with
camels

Bedouins live in
tents and herd
sheep and goats.

Empty Quarter

Coloured tiles on a reconstructed
Mesopotamian gateway.

Hookah pipe

## DESERT LIFE

The hot, dry climate of Southwest Asia
means that much of the region is desert.
Southern Saudi Arabia is covered by the world's
largest sandy desert, called the Empty Quarter. The only
people who live in this barren place are Bedouin nomads,
who use camels and now trucks to cross the desert.

Sana

YEMEN

## MUST SEE!

☑ PERSEPOLIS was capital of the Persian Empire in the
6th century BC. The ruins were uncovered in the
1930s. The palace walls have beautiful carvings.

☑ The KHALIFA TOWER in Dubai, UAE, is currently
the world's tallest building, rising 829 m high.
It was completed in 2009.

33

# NORTH ASIA

Three-quarters of Russia, the world's largest country, lies in Asia. The other quarter is in Europe. The Russian region of Siberia dominates North Asia. Only a third of Russia's people live here because of the harsh climate. Northern Asia also includes Kazakhstan, Uzbekistan, Turkmenistan, Tajikistan and Kyrgyzstan. These countries were part of a huge country called the Soviet Union until 1991, but are now independent. The main industries in North Asia are farming, forestry and mining. In the south, ancient trade routes cross the desert.

The flag of the Soviet Union.

## MUST SEE!

☑ REGISTAN SQUARE in the city of Samarqand is edged by beautiful Islamic buildings. Samarqand used to lie along the ancient Silk Road trade route.

☑ In Kazakhstan at spring and summer festivals you can see HORSE RACING, polo and displays of falconry. Wrestling is another traditional sport on the Russian steppes, or plains.

☑ The ARAL SEA in Kazakhstan was once a huge freshwater lake. Since the 1960s the rivers that feed it have been diverted to water nearby farmlands. The lake is now only a fraction of the size it was 60 years ago, and split into four.

Norilsk

Gas field

Russian Czar

**RUSSIA**

Ural Mountains

To Moscow

Cossacks

Horse racing

Yenisey river

Ob river

Russian Orthodox

Lake Ba

Fishing boat

Novosibirsk

**KAZAKHSTAN**

Astana

Registan Square

CASPIAN SEA

ARAL SEA

Bishkek

UZBEKISTAN

Tashkent

KYRGYZSTAN

TURKMENISTAN

Samarqand

Dushanbe

Ashgabat

TAJIKISTAN

Silk Road camels

## SILK ROUTE

The Silk Road was an ancient trade route that link China with western Asia and the Mediterranean. For hundreds of years, it was used to carry silk and spice from China all the way to Europe. Europeans did not know how to make silk, so the fabric was very precious. Lines of camels and donkeys crossed the barren land, calling at cities such as Samarqand, now in Uzbekistan.

# HISTORY ZONE
## RUSSIAN RULERS

Kings called czars ruled Russia from the late 1540s to early 1900s. However, in 1917 the last czar was overthrown and revolutionaries established a Communist government. From 1922 Russia became head of the Communist country called the Soviet Union. The Soviet Union broke up in 1991 and Russia has now formed a democratic-style government.

## ARCTIC OCEAN

## MINING

Siberia is rich in resources such as gold, diamonds, copper, oil, coal and natural gas. Russia is also the world's single biggest oil producer.

A Siberian coal mine.

## GRASSLAND NOMADS

On the grasslands of Kazakhstan, people traditionally live as nomads. They move their flocks of sheep or herds of horses in search of fresh grazing. They live in tents called gers or yurts, which are made of cloth or felt stretched over a wooden framework. These homes can be taken down and put up again quickly.

A Kazak herdsman packs up to move to new pastures for the summer.

*Icebreaker*

*Lena river*

*Factory*

**Yakutsk**

*Diamond mine*

*Balalaika*

*Oil field*

## S i b e r i a

*Bandy players*

## PACIFIC OCEAN

*Freight ship*

*Trans-Siberian Railway*

**Vladivostok**

## TRANS-SIBERIAN RAILWAY

The Trans-Siberian Railway is the world's longest railway line. Completed in 1916, it runs all the way from Moscow right across Asia to Vladivostok on the shores of the Pacific. This 9,288-km journey crosses eight time zones and takes eight days.

The Trans-Siberian Railway carries tourists as well as Russian passengers and goods.

# AFRICA

Incredible Africa is Earth's second-largest continent. Covering over 30 million sq km, it is made up of about a fifth of Earth's land area. Africa has many record-breaking features. The world's longest river and largest hot desert are located here. Africa is Earth's hottest continent, with temperatures rising to a sizzling 50 °C. It also has the second-largest rainforest, and huge areas of savannah grassland. In the east, the Great Rift Valley contains several vast lakes. Africa is home to the greatest wildlife show on Earth. The largest, heaviest and tallest land animals live here, along with many creatures found nowhere else.

## MOUNT KILIMANJARO

Africa's highest mountain, Kilimanjaro, rises to 5,895 m. Located in Tanzania, east Africa, this dormant volcanic mountain has three volcanic cones. Despite lying close to the Equator, it is snow-capped all year around. Hikers take five to seven days to scale this towering peak.

Climbers first reached the summit of Mt Kilimanjaro in 1889.

## SAVANNAH WILDLIFE

The hot, dry grasslands, or savannah, of east Africa are home to vast herds of grazing animals. Thousands of zebras, antelopes and wildebeest wander the plains in search of fresh grazing. They are stalked by lions, cheetahs and hyenas. You can also see elephants, giraffes and black rhinos. Tourists go on wildlife safaris, either in jeeps or in hot-air balloons.

A male lion strides through African grassland.

## SAHARA DESERT

Earth's largest hot desert, the Sahara covers a third of Africa – an area about the size of the USA. Temperatures rise to 50 °C by day but drop to freezing at night. About one quarter of this vast desert is sand dunes, the rest is rocky hills or stony plains. Two other large deserts, the Kalahari and Namib deserts, lie in southern Africa.

Sand dunes and rocky hills in the Sahara Desert.

## AFRICA FACT FILE

**HIGHEST PEAK:**
Mt Kilimanjaro: 5,895 m
**LONGEST RIVER:**
Nile: 6,695 km
**LARGEST LAKE:**
Lake Victoria: 68,800 sq km
**DESERT:**

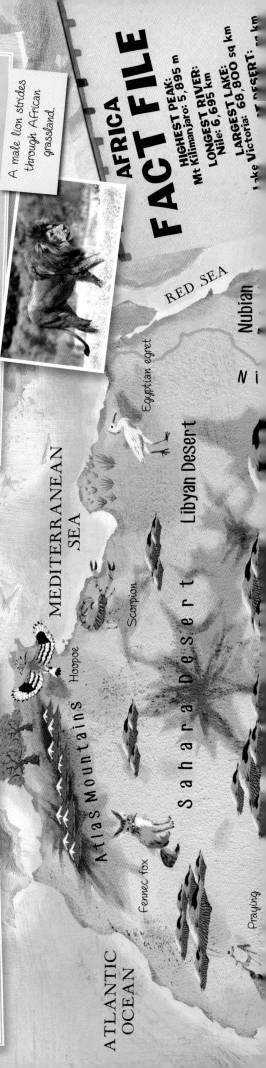

RED SEA

MEDITERRANEAN SEA

Egyptian egret

Nubian

Ni

Hoopoe

Scorpion

Libyan Desert

Atlas Mountains

Sahara Desert

Fennec fox

Praying

ATLANTIC OCEAN

Horn of Africa

Equator

## INDIAN OCEAN

Octopus

MADAGASCAR

Giraffe

Ethiopian Highlands

Mt Kilimanjaro

e Nile

Blue Nile

Lake Victoria

Ngorongoro Crater

Great Rift Valley

Zebra

Zambezi river

Termite mound

Congo river

Victoria Falls

Cheetah

Tugela Falls

r

Duker

African elephant

Okavango Delta

Kalahari Desert

Table Mountain

Crocodile

Chimpanzee

Namib Desert

er river

Pygmy hippo

Black-and-white Colobus monkey

### NATURAL WONDERS

* The Zambezi river drops 128 m at Victoria Falls on the boundary between Zambia and Zimbabwe. It is the world's greatest single curtain of falling water.

* Ngorongoro Crater in Tanzania is an ancient volcanic crater with amazing wildlife.

* Okavango Delta in Botswana is a vast swamp covering 15,000 sq km. This huge wetland is home to 60,000 antelope.

The lush banks of the Nile river in Egypt.

### RIVER NILE

Earth's longest river – the Nile – flows 6,695 km from the highlands of east Africa north to the Mediterranean. In Egypt and Sudan, the river creates a narrow ribbon of fertile farmland as it flows through the barren desert. It ends in a large, swampy delta draining into the Mediterranean Sea.

Mountain gorillas are endangered because of hunting.

### LANDSCAPE KEY

Areas of high ground

Tropical rainforest

Major mountain ranges

Desert

Savannah grassland

Dry, warm climate with plants such as olive trees

### RAINFOREST LIFE

A large area of tropical rainforest fills the basin of the Congo river in central Africa. These dense forests are home to elephants, leopards and tiny antelopes called duikers. There are also chimpanzees and relatives of the giraffe called okapi. Mountain gorillas inhabit the highlands of Uganda and Rwanda to the east.

# HISTORY ZONE

## ANCIENT EGYPT

Five thousand years ago, one of the world's earliest and greatest civilizations grew up along the banks of the Nile river in Egypt. The ancient Egyptians used the river's water to create fertile farmland. They built amazing temples and the colossal pyramid tombs of Giza, near Cairo, which still stand. The largest, the Great Pyramid, is made of 2.3 million huge limestone blocks and stands 139 m tall.

The Pyramids at Giza.

# THE SOUK

Many North African towns and cities have a large open-air market known as a 'souk'. These busy places are crowded with traders selling foods and spices and traditional handicrafts such as leather goods and handwoven carpets. Usually there are no set prices for goods and the buyer and seller agree on a price by haggling, or bargaining.

A crowded market in Morocco.

# MUST SEE!

The Roman ruins at LEPTIS MAGNA in Libya, and Carthage in Tunisia, date from the 1st century BC when parts of North Africa were a Roman colony (see p.49).

The GREAT MOSQUE in Timbuktu, Mali, is built of clay, straw and wood.

At the holy town of LALIBELA in Ethiopia, Christian churches have been cut into rock.

Madeira (PORTUGAL)

Canary Islands (SPAIN)

**MOROCCO**

Rabat

ATLAS MOUNTAINS

Algiers

Tunis

**TUNISIA**

Tripoli

MEDITERRANEAN SEA

Suez Canal

Date palms

Spices

Leptis Magna ruins

**ALGERIA**

SAHARA DESERT

**LIBYA**

**EGYPT**

Laayoune

Western Sahara (CLAIMED BY MOROCCO)

Orange tree

Abu Simbel temples

Mosque

**MALI**

Tuareg nomads

**NIGER**

Drummer

Traditional house

Nouakchott

Great Mosque

**CHAD**

**SUDAN**

CAPE VERDE

**MAURITANIA**

Timbuktu

Niger river

Kogiri instrument

Lake Chad

Dakar

**SENEGAL**

THE GAMBIA

Bamako

Niamey

Ndjamena

Praia

Banjul

Bissau

**GUINEA-BISSAU**

**GUINEA**

**BURKINA FASO**

Ouagadougou

Food market

**NIGERIA**

Conakry

**SIERRA LEONE**

Freetown

**IVORY COAST**

GHANA

BENIN

TOGO

Abuja

**CENTRAL AFRICAN REPUBLIC**

**SOUTH SUDAN**

**LIBERIA**

Yamoussoukro

Porto-Novo

Monrovia

Accra

Lomé

**CAMEROON**

Bangui

Malabo

Yaoundé

EQUATORIAL GUINEA

# NORTH AFRICA

North Africa covers a huge area, stretching 7,400 km from the Atlantic, eastwards to the Horn of Africa, and southwards from the Mediterranean Sea to Cameroon, South Sudan and Somalia. The Sahara Desert spreads right across the region, but North Africa also has green forests, mighty rivers, grasslands and high mountains. Almost all of this vast area was controlled by European countries such as the United Kingdom, France and Italy from the 1800s to the mid-1900s, but by 1970 most countries were independent. The region has mineral wealth but relatively little fertile farmland. North Africa has a rich history and many different cultures. However drought, conflict, war and poverty make life difficult for many people today.

## SUEZ CANAL

The Suez Canal cuts across the Sinai Peninsula in Egypt to link the Mediterranean and Red Seas. This 193-km canal allows ships to pass between Europe and Asia. This saves a very long trip around southern Africa. The canal was completed in 1869.

The Suez Canal is one of the world's busiest shipping lanes.

## FARMING

Much of North Africa is too dry for farming, but dates, olives and citrus fruit grow along the Mediterranean coast. Further south, Africa's hot, wet climate is suitable for growing peanuts, coffee and oil palms. West Africa produces over 60 per cent of the world's cocoa, which is used for making chocolate.

Orange harvesting in North Africa.

## DESERT NOMADS

Very few people inhabit the sandy wastes of the Sahara, but a nomadic people called the Tuareg have lived there for centuries. The Tuareg keep camels, which are used to cross the desert and also provide milk, meat and hides.

The Tuareg nomads are skilled camel riders.

## MUSLIM FAITH

Islam is the main religion of North and East Africa. In the 600s AD, Arab armies swept right across the region, converting most Africans to the Muslim religion. Many towns and villages have a mosque, with its slim tower or minaret. Muslims are called to prayer five times a day.

Many mosques have a tall spire known as a 'minaret'.

RED SEA

ERITREA
● Asmara

artoum

libela
urch

DJIBOUTI
● Djibouti

Horn of Africa

● Addis Ababa

ETHIOPIA

Ancient cave paintings

Face paint

SOMALIA

Mogadishu
●

INDIAN OCEAN

# SOUTHERN AFRICA

Southern Africa forms a huge wedge-shaped piece of land between the Atlantic and Indian Oceans. Madagascar, the world's fourth-largest island, lies to the east. Southern Africa is a land of contrasts, with tropical rainforests and grasslands, dry woodlands, deserts and mountains. For several hundred years, the region was colonized by Europeans, but all countries are now independent. The area has incredible mineral wealth including gold, copper and diamonds. However, as in North Africa, conflict, drought and also flooding bring hardship. Southern Africa has sprawling cities, but two-thirds of its people live in the countryside.

## GOLD AND DIAMONDS

Mining brings great wealth to southern Africa. Gold and diamonds discovered near Johannesburg, South Africa, in the late 1800s made mine-owners extremely wealthy. South Africa has the world's deepest gold mines. It is a leading producer of diamonds and platinum. Copper is mined in Zambia and the Democratic Republic of Congo far to the north.

A shipwreck off the Skeleton Coast.

## BARREN DESERTS

The Namib Desert runs along the Atlantic coast. Most of the moisture here comes from fog that rolls in off the ocean. The shoreline is called the Skeleton Coast because so many sailors have been shipwrecked and died here. The bones of hunted whales and seals also once littered the shoreline. To the east, the Kalahari Desert is home to the San Bushmen, who traditionally live by hunting and gathering wild foods.

Uncut diamonds from South Africa.

Maasai warriors are famous for their jumping dance.

## GAME RESERVES

Southern Africa is famous for its game reserves. These areas of land are set aside to protect wild animals such as lions, leopards, elephants, rhino and buffalo. Rhinos and elephants are now scarce because so many have been killed for their horns or tusks. Armed rangers patrol the reserves to guard against poachers.

## HISTORY ZONE
### END OF APARTHEID

In 1994 Nelson Mandela became president of South Africa in the country's first fully democratic election. South Africa had been dominated by Europeans since the 1600s. In 1948 the white government introduced a system called apartheid, that separated white from non-white South Africans. Mandela was jailed for fighting this racist system. He spent 27 long years in prison before being released in 1990.

## THE MAASAI

The Maasai people of Kenya and Tanzania are just one of the many tribal groups from southern Africa. Traditionally, they are cattle-herders, who measure their wealth in cattle. Boys begin herding from a young age. The Maasai are famous for their colourful clothing and for the jumping dance performed by warriors.

School children visit a centre for orphaned baby elephants in Kenya.

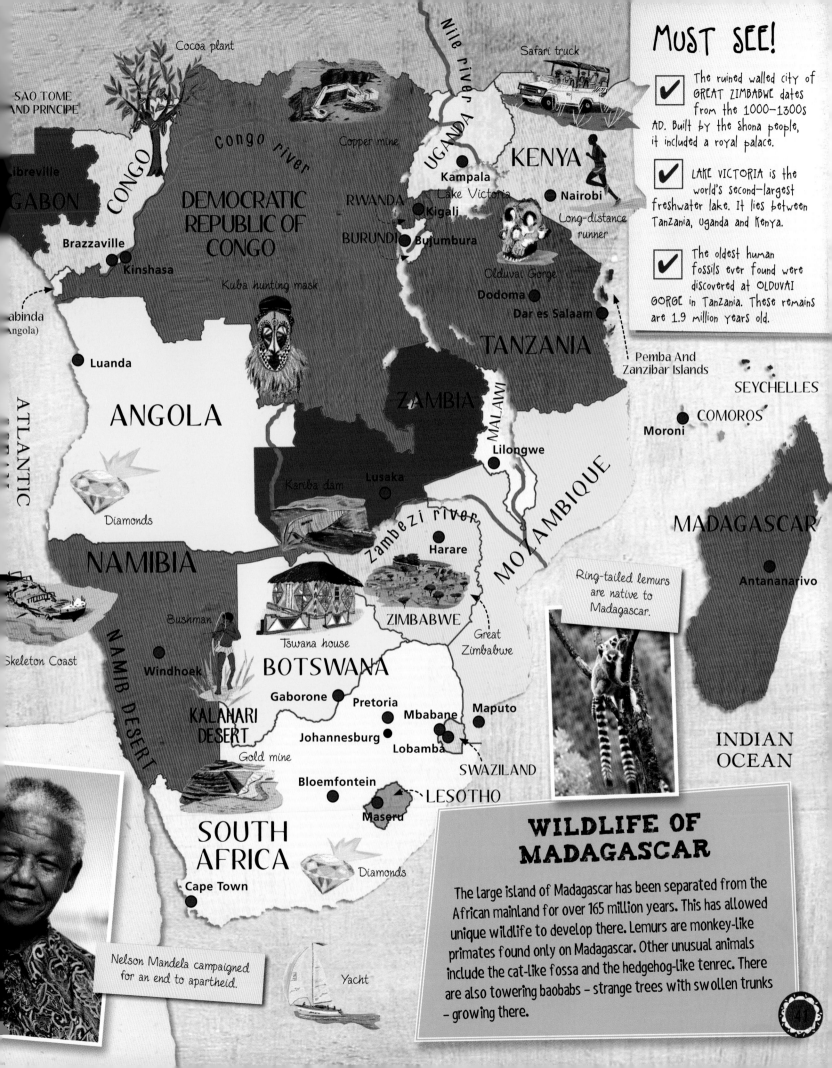

Cocoa plant

SAO TOME AND PRINCIPE

Libreville

GABON

CONGO

Congo river

Copper mine

Nile river

Safari truck

UGANDA

Kampala
Lake Victoria

KENYA

Nairobi

Long-distance runner

## MUST SEE!

✓ The ruined walled city of GREAT ZIMBABWE dates from the 1000–1300s AD. Built by the Shona people, it included a royal palace.

✓ LAKE VICTORIA is the world's second-largest freshwater lake. It lies between Tanzania, Uganda and Kenya.

✓ The oldest human fossils ever found were discovered at OLDUVAI GORGE in Tanzania. These remains are 1.9 million years old.

DEMOCRATIC REPUBLIC OF CONGO

RWANDA
Kigali

BURUNDI
Bujumbura

Brazzaville

Kinshasa

Kuba hunting mask

Olduvai Gorge

Dodoma

Dar es Salaam

TANZANIA

Pemba And Zanzibar Islands

Cabinda (Angola)

Luanda

ANGOLA

ATLANTIC

ZAMBIA

MALAWI

Lilongwe

SEYCHELLES

COMOROS
Moroni

Diamonds

Karíba dam

Lusaka

MOZAMBIQUE

NAMIBIA

Zambezi river

Harare

Bushman

Windhoek

NAMIB DESERT

Skeleton Coast

Tswana house

ZIMBABWE

Great Zimbabwe

MADAGASCAR

Antananarivo

Ring-tailed lemurs are native to Madagascar.

BOTSWANA

Gaborone

Pretoria

Mbabane

Maputo

KALAHARI DESERT

Johannesburg

Lobamba

SWAZILAND

INDIAN OCEAN

Gold mine

Bloemfontein

LESOTHO

Maseru

SOUTH AFRICA

Diamonds

Cape Town

Nelson Mandela campaigned for an end to apartheid.

Yacht

## WILDLIFE OF MADAGASCAR

The large island of Madagascar has been separated from the African mainland for over 165 million years. This has allowed unique wildlife to develop there. Lemurs are monkey-like primates found only on Madagascar. Other unusual animals include the cat-like fossa and the hedgehog-like tenrec. There are also towering baobabs – strange trees with swollen trunks – growing there.

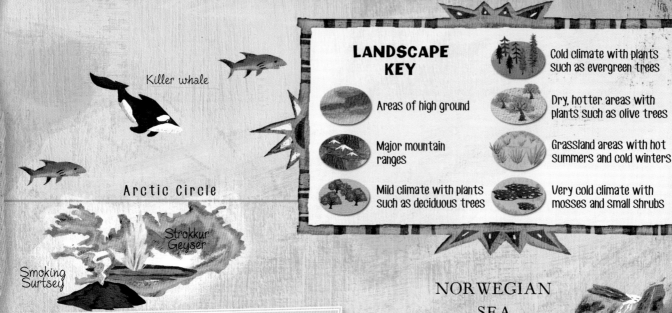

## LANDSCAPE KEY

Areas of high ground

Major mountain ranges

Mild climate with plants such as deciduous trees

Cold climate with plants such as evergreen trees

Dry, hotter areas with plants such as olive trees

Grassland areas with hot summers and cold winters

Very cold climate with mosses and small shrubs

Killer whale

Arctic Circle

Smoking Surtsey

Strokkur Geyser

# RAINFALL AND CLIMATE

Europe has a varied climate. Russia and Scandinavia are very cold in winter, while the Mediterranean region is warm and fairly dry. Westerly winds blowing off the Atlantic Ocean bring rain to western coasts. The same areas are warmed by a warm sea current called the Gulf Stream, which flows right across the Atlantic from the Gulf of Mexico.

ATLANTIC OCEAN

NORWEGIAN SEA

Fjords

Utigard waterfall

Green woodpecker

NORTH SEA

BAL SE

Cod

Elbe river

Badger

London

Rhine river

ENGLISH CHANNEL

Seine river

Danube r

Loire river

Matterhorn

BAY OF BISCAY

Red fox

Alps

Red squirrel

Garonne river

Alpine ibex

Wild

Ebro river

Rhone river

ADRIATIC

Tagus river

Pyrenees

Mt Vesuvius

 Seville

MEDITERRANEAN SEA

Mt Etna

## WEATHER REPORT

**Average temperature and rainfall figures:**

Jan: 5 °C
July: 18 °C
Jan: 50 mm
July: 40 mm

Jan: -7 °C
July: 19 °C
Jan: 50 mm
July: 85 mm

Jan: 10 °C
July: 28 °C
Jan: 48 mm
July: 5 mm

## RECORDS

Coldest place: Ust-Shchuger, Russia: -58 °C
Hottest place: Seville, Spain: 50 °C

# EUROPE

Spectacular Europe forms part of one great landmass with Asia. The two continents are separated by the Ural Mountains. Europe is the world's second smallest continent, only a fifth of the size of Asia. Europe has high mountains, sweeping river valleys and dense forests. Many areas of Europe that were once woodland are now farmland. Europe is the only continent with no deserts. Europe's coastline is very long and complicated, with many peninsulas and islands.

## VOLCANIC ICELAND

The island of Iceland sits on top of a volcanic ridge in the middle of the Atlantic Ocean. Iceland has 35 active volcanoes. There are also pools of bubbling mud and geysers – natural fountains which shoot jets of hot water high into the air. The water is heated by volcanic activity underground. Iceland is known as the 'Land of Ice and Fire'.

*Strokkur Geyser, Iceland.*

*The Mediterranean climate is sunny and dry.*

*The Danube river is a major trade route.*

## NATURAL WONDERS

* The Matterhorn is a beautiful steep-sided mountain in Switzerland. It stands 4,478 m high.

* Utigard Waterfall in Norway is one of the world's highest waterfalls.

* Strokkur Geyser on Iceland shoots a jet of boiling water 20 m high.

## ROLLING RIVERS

Europe's great rivers include the Volga, which runs over 3,600 km from Russia to the Caspian Sea. The River Danube flows from southern Germany to the Black Sea. The Rhine, which flows from the Alps to the North Sea, is a very busy waterway.

✳ London, UK

✳ Moscow, Russia

✳ Athens, Greece

# NORTHERN EUROPE

Northern Europe includes the island countries of Iceland, Ireland and the United Kingdom. The area known as Scandinavia is made up of Denmark, Norway and Sweden, with Finland to the east. Estonia, Latvia and Lithuania are known as the Baltic states. Northern parts of the region have a harsh climate, with long, dark, freezing winters. Many people live in the south or on the coast where the climate is milder. Most countries have relatively few people, but the United Kingdom is densely populated. The region has many modern industries and natural resources such as forests. In their leisure time, people enjoy sports such as soccer and skiing.

The Houses of Parliament in London, UK.

## TOP TOURISM

Tourism is a major industry in northern Europe. In the United Kingdom (UK), top attractions of the vibrant capital, London, include the Houses of Parliament. Tourists also visit the UK to watch plays written by famous playwright William Shakespeare (1564–1616). In Norway, cruise ships carry tourists to the spectacular fjords, deep inlets on the coast. The historic city of Tallinn in Estonia, with its old medieval centre, is also popular with tourists.

A replica of the *Rocket*, built by English engineer George Stephenson in 1829. It was one of the first steam locomotives.

## MIDNIGHT SUN

Parts of Norway, Sweden, Finland and Iceland are called the 'lands of the midnight sun'. The sun does not dip below the horizon here in midsummer, so it is light for 24 hours a day. In midwinter the sun does not rise, but skies are sometimes lit by an amazing natural light show called the Northern Lights.

## CHANGING TECHNOLOGY

The Industrial Revolution began in the United Kingdom in the mid 1700s with the invention of machines for spinning and weaving. The steam engine was also developed and was used first to transport goods and then people on the early railways. Iron, steel and later cars were made. Now high-tech industries are more important. In 1989, British scientist Tim Berners-Lee invented the World Wide Web, which revolutionized communications in the late 20th century.

The greenish-blue glow of the Northern Lights.

The Vikings sailed in elegant longships.

## HISTORY ZONE
### THE VIKINGS

The vikings of Scandinavia were a fierce warrior people who dominated Northern Europe from 700 to 1100 AD. Viking longships sailed from Denmark, Norway and Sweden to raid the coasts of Britain, France and Ireland. The word 'viking' means 'to go raiding'. The vikings colonized Iceland, Greenland and parts of Britain, France and Russia. These expert navigators even crossed the Atlantic to North America.

People bathing in a hot spring lake in Iceland.

# HOT SPRINGS

Volcanic activity in Iceland causes hot springs to bubble out of the ground. This energy is used to heat homes and provide electricity. People also bathe in lakes fed by hot springs.

# THE SAAMI

Northern Norway, Sweden and Finland are the land of the Lapps or Saami. These people traditionally lived by herding reindeer, which were reared for their meat, milk and hides. The Saami followed the reindeer as they moved north to Arctic tundra in summer, to graze on mosses and lichens, and then south to spend winter in sheltered forests.

A Saami herdsman dressed in traditional clothes.

Smoking volcano

**ICELAND**

**Reykjavik**

Fjord cruise ship

NORWEGIAN SEA

**SWEDEN**

Cross-country skier

Ice skates

Freight ship

Faroe Islands (Denmark)

Shetland Islands (UK)

Scotsman in a kilt

Wooden stave church

Dala wooden horse

**FINLAND**

**Helsinki**

**Tallinn**

**ESTONIA**

**NORWAY**
**Oslo**

**Stockholm**

**ATLANTIC OCEAN**

High stone cross

NORTH SEA

**UNITED KINGDOM**

**DENMARK**
**Copenhagen**

**Riga** **LATVIA**

BALTIC SEA

**LITHUANIA**
**Vilnius**

Little Mermaid statue

Latvian amber necklace

**Dublin**

London Eye

**IRELAND**

Stonehenge

**London**

ENGLISH CHANNEL

Yacht

Mackerel fish

# MUST SEE!

☑ The stone circle at STONEHENGE in southwest England, United Kingdom, was built about 4,000 years ago. The circle was probably used in ancient ceremonies to mark midsummer. Some of the stones are thought to come from hundreds of miles away – it's a mystery how they were transported.

☑ The statue of the LITTLE MERMAID in the harbour at Copenhagen, the Danish capital city, was inspired by the fairy tale by Danish writer Hans Christian Andersen, who wrote many stories famous the world over.

47

# STEEP-SIDED FJORDS

The coast of Norway is cut with deep, steep-sided inlets called fjords. Towering headlands on either side plunge down to the sea. These inlets were once coastal valleys which were carved by glaciers during the last Ice Age. When the ice melted, sea levels rose to flood the valleys.

The dramatic scenery of a Norwegian fjord.

# EUROPE FACT FILE

**HIGHEST PEAK:**
Mt Elbrus: 5,642 m

**LOWEST POINT:**
Shore of Caspian Sea:
28 m below sea level

**LONGEST RIVER:**
Volga: 3,692 km

**LARGEST LAKE:**
Caspian Sea: 371,000 sq km
[between Asia and Europe]

**LARGEST FRESHWATER LAKE:**
Ladoga, Russia: 17,700 sq km

**HIGHEST VOLCANO:**
Mt Etna: 3,329 m

The Jungfrau is a famous mountain in the Swiss Alps.

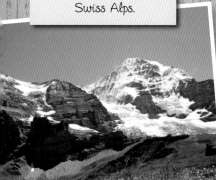

# SNOW-CAPPED PEAKS

Mountains run in an almost continuous arc across southern Europe, from the Pyrenees between France and Spain to the Alps and the Carpathians in the east. The Caucasus Mountains in Russia hold Europe's highest peak, Mount Elbrus. There are also peaks in Scotland and Scandinavia. Many mountains and other wild areas have been made into national parks and reserves.

# WILDLIFE WATCH

European woodlands are home to foxes, badgers, deer, boar and squirrels. Pine martens also build their dens here. The woods are also inhabited by birds such as owls and woodpeckers. Lynx and wolves can be seen in remote areas of northern and eastern Europe. The mountains are home to wild goats with long curving horns, called ibex.

# HOTSPOTS!

* Italy has many active volcanoes. Mount Etna on the island of Sicily has been erupting for hundreds of years. In 79 AD the eruption of Mount Vesuvius buried the Roman town of Pompeii in a thick layer of ash.

* In 1963 a volcanic eruption off Iceland caused a new island to rise from the sea. It was named Surtsey after the Icelandic god of fire.

N W E S

Reindeer

Eurasian lynx

Ust-Shchuger

Ural Mountains

Brown bear

Lake Ladoga

European wolf

Arctic Circle

Moscow

European pine marten

Common buzzard

Dneiper river

Volga river

Carpathian Mountains

Caucasus Mountains

Balkan ountains

BLACK SEA

Mt Elbrus

CASPIAN SEA

Balkan Whip snake

hens

AEGEAN SEA

Seal

The red fox is common in Europe's woodlands and is also seen in towns.

# WESTERN EUROPE

Western Europe stretches from Spain and Portugal eastwards to Germany and Italy. The region ranges from big countries such as France, to small states only the size of cities, such as San Marino. With a history reaching back over 2,000 years, the nations of western Europe have incredibly varied cultures and traditions. From the 1400s this region dominated much of the world, with colonies in the Americas, Asia and Africa, but now most of these former colonies are independent. For centuries, western Europe has been a world-famous centre for arts, science and inventions.

Germany produces high-tech sports cars.

## FARMING AND FOOD

A mild, wet climate makes the farmlands of western Europe highly fertile. Wheat, barley and potatoes are grown in the north. Tomatoes, olives and citrus fruit flourish in warm, dryer areas in the south. The Netherlands is famous for spring flowers. France, Germany, Italy, Spain and Portugal are major wine-producers. Belgium and Switzerland are known for fine chocolate, while France and Italy are famous for their cuisine.

A vineyard in France.

## EUROPEAN UNION

The European Union (EU) is a powerful economic and political alliance. With its headquarters in Brussels, it currently includes 27 countries across Europe. Seventeen of these share a single currency, the Euro. However, economic troubles since 2008 have hit some of these states hard.

The European Parliament building in Brussels, Belgium.

ENGLISH CHANNE

Mont Saint-Michel

Fishing boat

ATLANTIC OCEAN

Gar— river

Guggenheim Museum

Ebro river

Seafood paella (rice dish)

## MUST SEE!

☑ PARIS, capital of France, is known for its art galleries, museums, restaurants, cathedrals, artists' quarter and the famous Eiffel Tower, standing 324 m high.

☑ You'll need a boat to travel the watery 'streets' of VENICE in northeastern Italy. The city was built on a group of small islands and has over 400 bridges.

☑ The ancient Roman city of POMPEII near Naples, Italy, was buried by volcanic ash during an eruption of Mt Vesuvius in 79 AD. The site was excavated in the 1800s and now gives an amazing insight into Roman life.

PORTUGAL

Madrid

Tagus river

SPAIN

Lisbon

Olive trees

Flamenco dancer

Surfer

# CARS AND CLOCKS

[In] the 1800s, Germany has been a leading producer
[... ir]on, steel and machinery. Germany, France and Italy
[...] leading car manufacturers. Electronics,
[...ban]king and tourism are now
[... leadi]ng industries.
[... Swi]tzerland is famous
[... for] its banking industry
[... and] for making
[... cloc]ks.

**Amsterdam**

**The Hague**

NETHERLANDS

Rhine river

BELGIUM

**Brussels**

Chocolates

Eiffel Tower

**Paris**

[...]ne river

Artist

[...]re river

[FR]ANCE

Skier in the Alps

Rhone river

ANDORRA

Tour de France cyclists

Sagrada Familia church

Windsurfer

MEDITERRANEAN SEA

[Su]nbather

Balearic Islands (Spain)

BALTIC SEA

Brandenburg Gate

Spring flowers

Dachshund dog

**Berlin**

Elbe river

# GERMANY

LUXEMBOURG

**Luxembourg**

Neuschwanstein Castle

SWITZERLAND

LIECHTENSTEIN

**Bern**

A L P S

Gondola boat in Venice

**Milan**

Leaning Tower of Pisa

MONACO

SAN MARINO

ITALY

Corsica (France)

VATICAN CITY **Rome**

Sunbather

Sardinia (Italy)

Pizza

**Naples**

Pompeii

Sicily (Italy)

MALTA

# HISTORY ZONE

## THE ROMAN EMPIRE

From around 300 BC to 300 AD the world's greatest empire was centred on Rome, now in Italy. At its height the Roman Empire covered half of Europe and parts of the Middle East and North Africa. The Romans built paved roads, aqueducts to move water, and fine cities with public baths and theatres. They improved farming and technology throughout their empire.

The Roman Colosseum was a huge entertainment arena.

A football match in Spain.

# SPORT

The mountains, such as the Alps in western Europe, are centres for climbing, hiking, skiing and snow-boarding. Skaters glide over frozen ponds and waterways. Swimming, sailing and windsurfing are popular on lakes and Mediterranean beaches. The famous Tour de France cycle race crosses hills, plains and mountains. Soccer is the single most popular sport, with many Western European cities hosting world-class teams.

# THE ARTS

Italy and France are fashion capitals of the world. The latest styles of top designers are paraded on the catwalks of Paris and Milan. Western Europe has long been famous for the arts, including painting and sculpture.

A catwalk model at Paris Fashion Week.

W N E S

# EASTERN EUROPE

Eastern Europe covers a large area, stretching from the Arctic Ocean in the north, southwards to the Black Sea and Mediterranean. In the southeast, Greece, Serbia, Croatia, Bulgaria and Albania are all part of a region called the Balkans. The westernmost part of Russia, the largest country in the world, is also in Eastern Europe. Northern parts of the region are cold and dry, the south is hot in summer and mild and wet in winter. The region is famous for its beautiful forests, historic cities, agriculture and industry, mining and the arts.

## MUST SEE!

ST BASIL'S CATHEDRAL, Moscow, was built by the Russian czar, the Terrible in the mid-1500s. striped onion-shaped domes, this one of the most famous buildir the world. ✓

The BLUE MOSQUE in Istanbul i masterpiece of Islamic architec In medieval times, Istanbul was Constantinople and was an impo trading city straddling Europe ✓

BRAN CASTLE, in Transylvania, is said by some to be the ho vampire Count Dracula, a char created by Irish writer Bram ✓

## MUSIC AND DANCE

Two of the world's most famous ballet companies are based in western Russia: the Bolshoi Ballet of Moscow and the Kirov Ballet of St Petersburg. Classical ballet developed in the 1800s. The smooth, graceful movements demand great skill, strength and stamina. The mountainous state of Austria is known for its many classical music composers, including Mozart, Schubert and Strauss.

The famous Kirov Ballet goes on tours across the world.

Sugar beet farming in Poland.

## FARMING

Farming thrives on the rolling plains of Eastern Europe. Crops grown here include wheat, barley, sugar beet, sunflowers and potatoes. Cattle and pigs are also reared. Bulgaria is famous for rose growing. The petals are used to make perfume, soap and cosmetics. The rich, dark soil of Ukraine and Moldova is very fertile. Ukraine has been known as the 'bread basket' of Europe because of its vast agricultural fields.

## SPOTTY DOGS

Dalmatian dogs originally came from Croatia. The breed was developed to run beside carriages and fire engines. The spotted coat was easily recognized and helped clear the way of people. The breed became very popular, partly because of two Walt Disney films based on the book "The Hundred and One Dalmatians" by British author Dodie Smith.

A Dalmatian dog.

BALTIC SEA

RUSSIA

Famous scientist Marie Curie

Warsaw

Mozart

Prague castle

POLAND

Prague

CZECH REPUBLIC

SLOVAKIA

Bratislava

Vienna

Budapest

AUSTRIA

HUNGARY

Bran ca

SLOVENIA

Ljubljana

Zagreb

ROMAN

Danube Bucha

BOSNIA AND HERZEGOVINA

Belgrade

river

CROATIA

Sarajevo

SERBIA

BULGA

MONTENEGRO

KOSOVO

Pristina

Sofi

Podgorica

Skopje

MACEDONIA

Tirana

ALBANIA

GREECE

Ancient Greek Parthenon

Athens

MEDITERRANEAN SEA

ARCTIC OCEAN

Ural Mountains

Factory

Russian Blue cat

Mining

St Basil's Cathedral

t Petersburg

Mushrooms

Dnieper river

sk

Moscow

Spicy cabbage soup

RUSSIA

Yuri Gagarin, first man in space, 1961

LARUS

Kiev

Volga river

KRAINE

Tractor

Chisinau

Sunflowers

Russian nesting dolls

CASPIAN SEA

BLACK SEA

Blue Mosque

nbul

Ankara

TURKEY

nbather

Nicosia

CYPRUS

## POLITICAL CHANGE

The last 25 years have seen great changes in the governments of eastern Europe. Communist governments ruled much of the region from the end of World War II (1945) to the late 1980s. States such as Belarus, Ukraine and Moldova were part of a huge Communist country called the Soviet Union, which also included Russia. But many countries rejected Communism after 1990, and most now have democratic-style governments.

Belarusians celebrate Independence Day. Belarus became independent from the Soviet Union in 1991.

# HISTORY ZONE

## ANCIENT GREECE

Two and a half thousand years ago, Greece was the birthplace of European civilization. The ancient Greeks were great thinkers, architects and artists. They built fine cities with graceful temples decorated with marble statues. These ruined temples still stand in many parts of the ancient Greek world, including what is now Turkey, the island of Sicily and North Africa. Athens, the Greek capital, was the birthplace of democracy in about 500 BC.

Ancient Greek statues at the Acropolis, Athens.

51

# ANTARCTICA AND THE ARCTIC

Antarctica and the Arctic share a similar climate, with long, dark, bitterly cold winters. From space the two regions look similar, being covered with ice or snow. However they are also very different. The Arctic, which surrounds the North Pole, is mostly formed from ice-covered parts of the Arctic Ocean. Antarctica is a vast, icy continent, covering most of the southern polar region. It is Earth's fifth-largest continent – and also the most isolated. It was only discovered in the 1820s. Antarctica is the coldest, windiest place on Earth, with temperatures dropping to -80 °C. People have lived in the Arctic for thousands of years, while Antarctica has never been inhabited.

*Antarctic Peninsula*

Ronne She

## POLAR REGIONS

The Arctic lies in the far north and Antarctica lies in the far south of the planet. Imaginary lines known as the Arctic and Antarctic circles mark the limits of the polar areas.

The Arctic

Antarctica

Arctic Circle

Antarctic Circle

When one of the Poles is tilting towards the sun, it has summer and is bathed in sunlight 24 hours a day. At the same time, the opposite Pole is tilting away and experiencing 24-hour darkness.

Arctic terns breed in Greenland then migrate to Antarctica each year.

## THE ARCTIC

The area inside the Arctic Circle is mostly ocean, edged by Greenland and the most northerly parts of America, Europe and Asia. The Arctic Ocean is covered by a layer of ice which gets thicker in winter, when temperatures drop to -40° C. In summer some of this ice melts. The Arctic ice is is now getting thinner because of global warming. This is making life difficult for Arctic animals such as polar bears.

Shrimp

Polar bears hunt for seals on the Arctic ice caps.

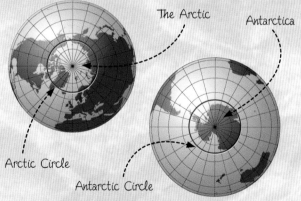

Midnight sun in Antarctica.

SOUTHERN OCEAN

Albatross

Blue whale

Antarctic
scientist

Emperor
penguin

# ANTARCTICA

Transantarctic Mountains

nson
assif

South
Pole

South Polar
Plateau

Storm petrel

Vostok
Research Station
(Russian)

Ross Ice
Shelf

McMurdo
Research Station
(USA)

The Ross Ice shelf is
750 m thick in places.

Starfish

Seal

## HISTORY ZONE
### ANTARCTIC TREATY

In the mid-1900s many countries claimed
land in Antarctica. In 1959 these claims
were set aside as countries signed the
Antarctic Treaty. This declared that the
continent should be used only for peaceful
purposes, such as science. No one is allowed
to live there permanently, and no mining
is permitted. The treaty protects this icy
wilderness and its wildlife. McMurdo Station
is the largest research base in Antarctica.
It is operated by US scientists.

### LANDSCAPE KEY

Bitterly cold
climate with
snow and ice

Mountain range

Ice shelf

Emperor penguins
live in the
Antarctic seas.

## ANTARCTIC ICE

Antarctica is Earth's highest continent. This is
because it is covered by a thick cap of ice, up to
4.8 km deep in places. Ice very slowly flows down
from high ground to the sea, forming glaciers. At the
coast the glaciers forms floating ice shelves, and also
icebergs. The Ross Ice Shelf is roughly the size of France.

## WILDLIFE WATCH

The climate of Antarctica is too
harsh for animals to live inland. Seals
and seabirds, including penguins,
breed on the coast in large numbers.
The seas around Antarctica are rich
in wildlife including fish, shrimp,
starfish and whales.

53

# OCEANS

Earth has five great oceans and many smaller seas. All the oceans are connected – water from the oceans continually circulates around the world. Together the oceans and seas cover 71 per cent of the planet's surface and hold 97 per cent of all its water. Moisture from the oceans rises into the air where it forms clouds, which shed rain, returning water to the oceans. This endless cycle also brings rain to the dry land. Ocean water is always on the move, due to waves, tides and currents. Winds blowing across the sea surface create waves, while tides are mainly caused by the pull of the Moon's gravity on the oceans.

## OCEANS FACT FILE

**PACIFIC OCEAN:**
Earth's largest ocean covers about 166,241,000 sq km – more than one third of the planet's surface. This enormous ocean is edged by a ring of volcanoes called the Ring of Fire.

**ATLANTIC OCEAN:**
The Atlantic covers about 106,400,000 sq km. This relatively young ocean only started to form 180 million years ago!

**INDIAN OCEAN:**
Earth's third-largest ocean covers about 73,556,000 sq km. From time to time, tropical storms called cyclones sweep in from the ocean to devastate the coasts of India and Bangladesh.

**SOUTHERN OCEAN:**
The icy waters around Antarctica are called the Southern Ocean. Covering about 20,327,000 sq km, these are the world's stormiest seas.

**ARCTIC OCEAN:**
Earth's smallest ocean lies in the far north. Covering about 14,056,000 sq km, it is topped with pack ice. Icebergs floating south from the Arctic are a hazard in warmer seas.

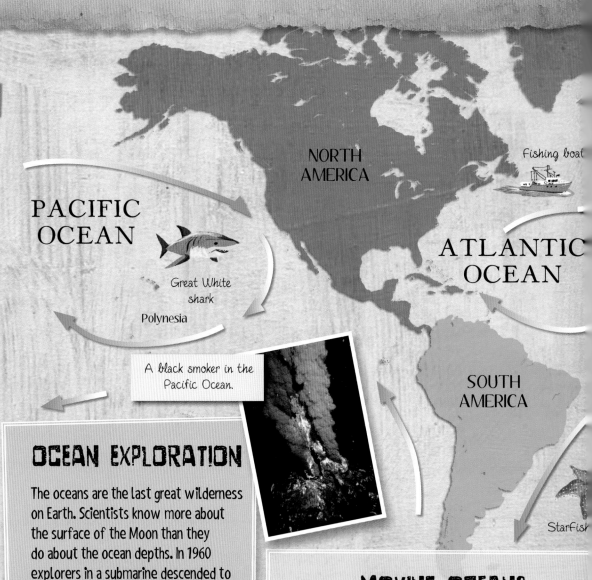

NORTH AMERICA

PACIFIC OCEAN

Great White shark

Polynesia

Fishing boat

ATLANTIC OCEAN

SOUTH AMERICA

Starfish

A black smoker in the Pacific Ocean.

## OCEAN EXPLORATION

The oceans are the last great wilderness on Earth. Scientists know more about the surface of the Moon than they do about the ocean depths. In 1960 explorers in a submarine descended to Earth's deepest point, Challenger Deep in the Pacific, 11 km below the surface. In 1977 scientists discovered weird chimneys called black smokers on the ocean bed. These volcanic chimneys release black clouds of super hot, mineral-rich water.

## MOVING OCEANS

The salt water in seas and oceans is always moving. Wind create surface currents which flow around in giant circles. The water flows clockwise in the northern hemisphere and anti-clockwise in the southern hemisphere. Ocean currents help to spread the Sun's heat around the globe.

# OCEAN FOOD CHAINS

[th]e survival of all life in the oceans depends on microscopic plants and [ani]mals called plankton. These tiny plants and animals float at the surface [of] the water. They are eaten by small creatures such as shrimp (as well [as] some big sea animals). Shrimp are in turn eaten by larger animals such as [fis]h. Fish are preyed on by top predators, such as sharks.

A magnified picture of plankton. Plankton floats on the ocean surface.

Great White sharks are top predators of the seas.

## ARCTIC OCEAN

Icebreaker boat

Killer whale

ASIA

EUROPE

Blue whale

AFRICA

**KEY**

Major ocean current

X Challenger Deep

Micronesia

Yacht

Cyclone

Melanesia

Polynesia

### INDIAN OCEAN

OCEANIA

### PACIFIC OCEAN

Angel Fish

Pacific Islanders are skilled fishermen.

## SOUTHERN OCEAN

[s]torm petrel

# OCEANIA

Earth's largest ocean, the Pacific, stretches halfway around the globe. Thousands of islands are scattered across this vast ocean. These islands, together with Australia, New Zealand and New Guinea form a region known as Oceania. The Pacific Islands are divided into three main groups: Melanesia, Micronesia and Polynesia. Many Pacific Islanders depend on the sea for food.

ANTARCTICA

# FLAGS OF THE WORLD